Jellyfish

Animal
Series editor: Jonathan Burt

Jellyfish

Peter Williams

REAKTION BOOKS

Published by
REAKTION BOOKS LTD
Unit 32, Waterside
44–48 Wharf Road
London N1 7UX, UK
www.reaktionbooks.co.uk

First published 2020, reprinted 2020
Copyright © Peter Williams 2020

Printed and bound in India by Replika Press Pvt. Ltd

A catalogue record for this book is available from the British Library

ISBN 978 1 78914 215 0

Contents

Introduction

The evolutionary biologist Matt Wilkinson has compared a jelly-fish to an embarrassing uncle no one likes to discuss: without a head or brain, with a mouth that doubles as an anus and bearing little resemblance to other animals.[1] Largely ignored, perceived as alien creatures and best avoided, jellyfish nevertheless have the power to fascinate. Whether it is their gentle pulsation through a column of water or the sheer beauty of their translucent bells and long, trailing tentacles, there is surely something mesmeric about these ancient creatures that frequently invade our shores.

Found from pole to tropic, close to the surface of our coastal waters as well as deep in the abyssal depths of the oceans, they form an important part of the sea's plankton and vary in size from the gigantic to the minute. One of the largest, Nomura's jellyfish, which can measure 1.8 m (6 ft) across its bell, has caused fishing boats to capsize when accidentally caught in their nets. The majority of jellyfish worldwide are much smaller, most less than 2.5 cm (1 in.) in diameter, though their tentacles can be considerably longer. Size is not a measure of safety when it comes to being stung by one, however. The Irukandji jellyfish, which happens to be the most venomous of all species of jellyfish, measures just 1.3 cm (½ in.) across when fully grown, but has tentacles that can reach 1 m (3 ft) in length. The clinging jellyfish, *Gonionemus vertens*, which is only a little larger, can likewise give

The lion's mane jellyfish, *Cyanea capillata*, photographed by Alexander Semenov, 2009.

7

an unpleasant, though not lethal, sting. Curiously, its toxicity varies according to where it is found in the world. Even then, responses to its sting range from mild to severe.

We refer to these animals as 'jellyfish' because of the gelatinous nature of their connective tissue, or mesoglea, that separates the two cell layers that make up their body wall, an outer ectoderm and an inner endoderm. The commonly described free-floating jellyfish is also known by the name 'medusa'. Typically, it has the shape of a bell or umbrella, the underside of which has a central structure known as a manubrium, at the end of which is a mouth. Arising from the margin of the bell, as well as around the mouth, are normally tentacles bearing stinging cells known as nematocysts, used for capturing and subduing prey. There is

Arguably the largest jellyfish: Nomura's. Found off the coast of South Korea.

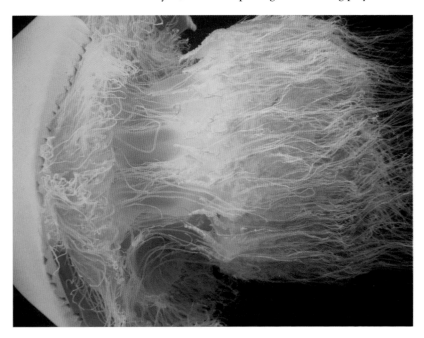

great diversity in shape, size and colour among jellyfish but this description serves as an introduction to those commonly seen in coastal waters. Many that inhabit the deeper recesses of the ocean have less typical shapes.

The clinging jellyfish, *Gonionemus vertens*. Small, but with a powerful sting.

The poet Jean Sprackland rightly observes the word jellyfish is faintly comical, conjuring up something wobbly in waxed paper bowls, often associated with children's parties.[2] As if to reinforce this playful image, the Welsh slang term for a jellyfish is *pysgod wibbly wobbly*. Removed from its watery environment, a jellyfish assumes an amorphous shape not unlike a blancmange. Gone are the delicate tentacles, the frills and subtle colours. Like some regurgitated eel, it sits motionless on the sand, glistening in the sun, inviting speculation as to what it might be. Indeed, Tom Fort's description of an eel, 'a creature of mystery . . . with few admirers and fewer friends', might equally apply to a beached

9

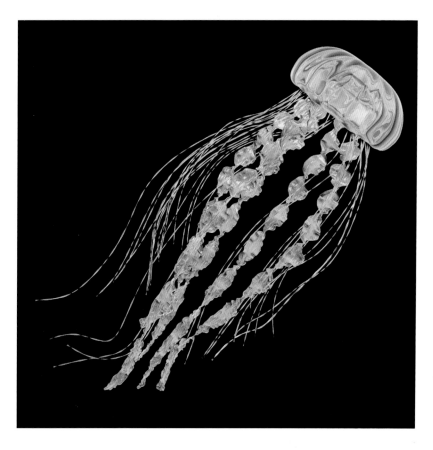

jellyfish.[3] It is extraordinary how transformed the animal is when viewed from beneath the surface of the sea. Here, in its watery element, it radiates beauty, fragility and elegance.

While our knowledge of the ocean's currents and tides stretches back a long way, our understanding of what forms of life exists below the surface of the water is still in its infancy, and then mostly confined to the topmost layer of the sea where light can penetrate. As far back as the third century BC, Alexander the Great commissioned a glass diving bell to be built so that he could witness life underwater for himself. Accounts of what he saw vary, but the gentle pulsing of jellyfish must surely have caught his attention, as well as the sheer variety of other forms of marine life. Of the gelatinous creatures to be found below the water, we are able to distinguish two main groups of jellyfish, the Cnidaria and the Ctenophora. Some people widen the definition further to include salps, otherwise known as tunicates, which pump water through one end of their bodies and expel it at the other end. Here, I will confine myself to the first two groupings.

Within the phylum Cnidaria, which also includes sea anemones and corals, can be distinguished three classes of jellyfish: the Scyphozoa or 'true' jellyfish; the Hydrozoa, which can be small and solitary or large and colonial in their habit; and the Cubozoa, or box jellyfish, the extremely venomous ones. Ctenophores or comb jellies constitute the other division of jellyfish, but these belong to the separate phylum Ctenophora.

Cnidarians typically possess stinging cells or nematocysts, used both as a means of self-defence and as a way of killing or immobilizing prey they come into contact with. Ctenophores, on the other hand, lack stinging cells but instead possess colloblasts, which are sticky threads used to entrap their prey. Like nematocysts, colloblasts are specialized cells, each containing tightly coiled threads within a capsule that can be shot out at high velocity. Another feature that distinguishes ctenophores from cnidarians is their through-gut, in other words a mouth and an anus that are separate and connected to one another. They also tend to deviate from the typical bell appearance of a medusa. They are either oval in shape, or have large lobes, or their bodies are compressed into a flattened band. Some have tentacles, others don't. One, called Venus's girdle, is in the shape of ribbon,

about 1 m (40 in.) long and 5 cm (2 in.) wide, with well-developed muscles which allow it to swim with an undulating motion in the water.

Jellyfish come from an ancient lineage. It was initially thought that the Ediacara Hills of South Australia contained impressions of jellyfish in the fine-grained sandstone. However, many of these disc fossils appear to have rooting structures, suggesting the impressions in the sediment are more likely of plants. Other fossils found there may indeed be primitive, soft-bodied representatives of early cnidarians or their predecessors, but the first unequivocal medusa puts in an appearance some time later, in the Cambrian period, when there was an explosion of different forms of life. One early Cambrian fossil named *Olovooides*, from about 530 million years ago, appears to show a sequence of developmental stages which resemble juvenile medusae.[4] It may represent the stem group for all 'true' jellyfish. As far as ctenophores are concerned, there is one organism known from the Ediacaran period, called *Eoandromeda octobranchiata*, which has been interpreted as a possible stem group for comb jellies.[5] We are talking here about very early life forms; animals that lack fluid-filled cavities or coeloms, found in most invertebrates. As to which is the most primitive invertebrate, the comb jelly or the sponge, there is no agreement, but it seems likely that one or the other is the sister to all other lineages of multicellular animals.[6]

Whatever their origins, jellyfish make up a very successful and diverse group of animals, if a somewhat neglected one. I have chosen to begin with a history of jellyfish, from earliest times to the present, focusing on the challenges they have posed to those who sought to position them in the natural world in relation to other life forms. In the first chapter I also delve into the jellyfish's life cycle, which is more complicated than one might suppose. What we recognize as a jellyfish is normally the free-floating,

Sixteenth-century painting of Alexander the Great, lowered in a glass diving bell.

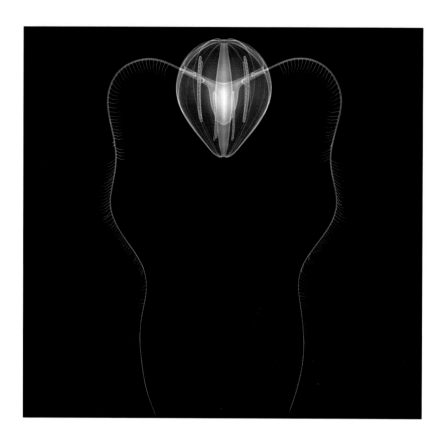

Illustration of a comb jelly by the artist known as 'Ctenophor', 2018.

pelagic stage in the life cycle, otherwise known as the 'medusa', but this commonly derives from a polyp which itself is fixed to a surface and therefore sessile. There is, in other words, an 'alternation of generations' in the jellyfish life cycle, one a sexual phase, the other an asexual one. As well as having a polyp and a medusa stage, there is also an egg and a free-floating planula to consider. In the second chapter, the relationship we have with these creatures is explored in some depth. I suggest attitudes towards

Dickinsonia costata, a possible fossil precursor to jellyfish.

jellyfish have been coloured by the uncertainty and ambiguity they generate in us, and also by their potential to cause us harm. Some of the mythology surrounding the term 'medusa' is also examined, along with the experience of being in close contact with these creatures in their watery environment. The sheer variety of jellyfish within the zooplankton forms the subject matter of Chapter Three. They range from tiny, solitary forms to large, colonial ones, like the Portuguese man-of-war, to light-diffracting comb jellies, and finally to bioluminescent creatures that inhabit the abyssal depths of the oceans. Chapter Four is devoted to the ways jellyfish have been represented by illustrators and by those working in other media, and how technology has advanced so that we have moving images of jellyfish, some from environments where no natural light can penetrate. In Chapter Five I look at jellyfish from a cultural perspective and ask what inspiration they have provided to writers, artists and architects. I also take a look at jellyfish cuisine, its origins, and how eating jellyfish may become a thing of the future. The contribution certain jellyfish have made and are currently making to humanity is explored in Chapter Six. In the jellyfish *Turritopsis dohrnii*, nature has provided us with an example of an immortal animal, giving us the opportunity to examine those factors that might promote longevity, while within the jellyfish *Aequorea victoria* is contained a chemical called green fluorescent protein that is proving useful in studying brain function and cancer growth. Finally, in Chapter Seven, I look at jellyfish in profusion, as blooms, and explore whether these might be indicators of climate change and whether or not the numbers of jellyfish in the sea are expanding. If indeed we are experiencing a renaissance of jellyfish, are we to expect, as one scientist has predicted, a change in the oceans towards a gelatinous future or are we simply seeing fluctuations in jellyfish numbers over a long time scale?

By the end of the book I hope to have convinced the reader that jellyfish deserve more of our attention than has been the case hitherto, since, as well as being undeniably problematical to us at times, they can also be of use to us in several beneficial ways, and even cast new light on the evolution of animal life on our planet.

1   A Lineage of Uncertainty

What have we here? A man or a fish? Dead or alive?
Shakespeare, *The Tempest*

An aura of uncertainty surrounds jellyfish. The word itself is ambiguous. Fish they certainly are not. They have no backbone, indeed no skeleton of any sort. Yet they co-exist with creatures possessing backbones, such as fish, and are capable of moving in the water as a result of a series of propulsive efforts. Jelly-like they certainly are, made largely of a translucent material which starts to dissolve as soon as it is out of water. The delicacy of their structure only becomes apparent to those willing to observe them from below the surface of the water, or who have access to a microscope.

Aristotle, who spent several years living on the Aegean coast, was accustomed to seeing jellyfish in the waters there. He gave them the name 'Acalephs' from the Greek meaning nettle, drawing attention to an important distinguishing feature of the group, namely their ability to sting or irritate the skin.[1] They are still known in some quarters as 'sea nettles'. Jellyfish clearly puzzled Aristotle. Were they plants, animals, or perhaps some intermediate living thing? As far as Aristotle was concerned, to qualify as an animal they needed a digestive system, blood vessels, a sense of touch and the ability to move independently. It wasn't necessary for all these attributes to be present, only a few, yet the jellyfish posed a conundrum. While possessing a mouth, there was no separate exit for waste matter, the mouth serving as a transit

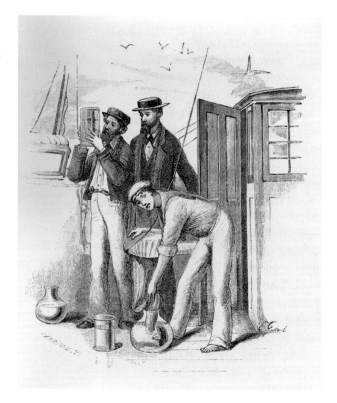

point for food and waste. No blood vessels could be seen. On the other hand, the jellyfish did appear to be sensitive to objects it came into contact with and, to use Aristotle's own words, 'used the asperity of its body as protection against its enemies'. Much of its movement in the water appeared passive but, despite being at the mercy of the waves and currents, it was certainly able to pulse up and down a column of seawater.

In conclusion, the jellyfish fulfilled some of the qualifications of an animal, but not all. Could it therefore be a plant? One distinction Aristotle drew between animals and plants was that animals reproduced sexually while plants did not, and he saw no clear evidence of a sexual life history in jellyfish. To him, they were an enigmatic form of life and jellyfish have remained something of a puzzle ever since. The designation *incertae sedis*, meaning 'of uncertain status', certainly applied early on, but even now there is a measure of doubt as to where jellyfish came from and what their nearest relatives are.

The influence of Aristotle's thinking on matters relating to natural history cannot be overstated. His writings on jellyfish, along with his observations on other inhabitants of the sea, were the earliest recorded attempts to describe these creatures. To him they were 'imperfect' and that 'imperfection' meant they were assigned a lowly position in the chain of being, on a par with sponges, another enigmatic group.

Since Aristotle's time, other observers have found it equally difficult to classify jellyfish. Pliny the Elder saw them, along with sea urchins and sponges, as having features of both animals and plants, a view that persisted until the eighteenth century. Even the great classifier of nature Carl Linnaeus allocated them to a group he called 'zoophytes' ('zoo-' meaning animal and 'phyte-' meaning plant), offering little clarity as to what they were. In his *Systema naturae* of 1735, the term 'zoophyte' was used to describe creatures that inhabited the shadowy world between the two major kingdoms. Linnaeus even used botanical terms to describe some parts of a jellyfish, while drawing parallels between their bodies and those of molluscs, which were unequivocally animals.

Of course, jellyfish weren't the only zoophytes. Other life forms fell into the category too: corals, starfish, polyps and sea anemones, for example. As Susannah Gibson in her book *Animal, Vegetable, Mineral?* points out, they raised a number of issues for the early naturalists. As well as calling into question the definitions of 'plant' and 'animal' and the relationship between the two, they posed a problem as to where they belonged in what was then regarded as a divinely ordered chain connecting all living things.[2] The notable French naturalist Georges-Louis Leclerc, comte de Buffon, came to the conclusion that there was no absolute distinction between plants and animals, merely a continuum of life. Jellyfish fitted into the 'in-between zone'. 'Nature', he argued, 'proceeded by imperceptible degrees from the most perfect to the most imperfect animal and from that to the vegetable.'[3] Oliver Goldsmith, in his *Animated Nature*, described jellyfish as being 'nauseous and despicable creatures that excite our curiosity by their imperfections'.[4] Perhaps it was these very 'imperfections' that made people hesitate about allocating them to a particular group.

The naturalists who really laid the foundations for understanding zoophytes, and therefore jellyfish, were a disparate group of little-known individuals, enthusiasts with enquiring minds and powers of observation, who were prepared, individually, to investigate this neglected 'imperfect' group. Later, as we shall see, the story was taken up by some of the better-known figures in the world of science, scientists such as Agassiz, Huxley and Haeckel. They built on the knowledge of these early naturalists, and their own conclusions and thought processes often reflected their beliefs about the natural world.

Our story begins with an enquiry into two zoophytes that proved to be close relatives of the jellyfish, namely corals and polyps. A young French physician, Jean-André Peyssonnel, had been observing different types of coral in the Bay of Marseilles. From their stony structure would emerge 'flowers', not dissimilar to small, upturned jellyfish (the term 'flower' was used because corals were at that time regarded either as plants or a hybrid of plant and mineral material). These 'flowers' responded to touch by drawing in their 'petals'. Peyssonnel was able to isolate these 'flowers' within the pores in the coral and came to the conclusion that they were 'insects', in other words, animals (any small invertebrate animal at that time was termed an 'insect').[5] His *Dissertation sur le corail* was brought to the attention of the Académie des Sciences in Paris, but unfortunately the study was overlooked (perhaps he was too junior) until a Swiss naturalist, Abraham Trembley, studying a freshwater relative of coral, the polyp *Hydra*, noticed the contractility of the polyp's body, its response to touch and its ability to turn head-over-heels. Trembley wrote:

> Thinking that the polyps were plants, I could hardly imagine that the movements of those slender threads located at one end of their bodies were their own. Yet they appeared to move by themselves and not at all as a response to the agitation in the water.[6]

The 'threads' resembled the 'petals' observed earlier in coral by Peyssonnel. In fact, what both men had observed were tentacles, shorter but otherwise not dissimilar to the tentacles of a jellyfish. Trembley's voice was heard. Peyssonnel's observations were repeated and his findings vindicated. At last, the polyp and the coral's animal nature were established beyond doubt and it didn't take long before a relationship between the polyp, the coral and the jellyfish was established too. Importantly, all had tentacles and soft bodies, and were capable of showing some independent motion. They also displayed a radial symmetry. In other words, they shared a body plan in which each individual could be divided into similar halves by passing a plane at any angle along a central axis. It was this particular feature that persuaded a German naturalist, Johann Friedrich von Eschscholtz, to group all three together. He also included starfish in with the polyps, corals and jellyfish. The great French naturalist Georges Cuvier accorded

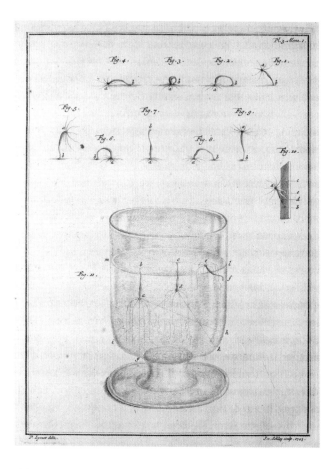

this group a separate 'embranchement' in his classification of animals based on similarities in their body plan. Because of their radial symmetry, he designated the group the 'Radiata', one of four primary divisions of animals in his *Le Règne animal* of 1817. As the historian Mary Winsor points out, the 'Radiata' were, to a large extent, 'leftovers', animals that did not particularly share many positive characteristics but found themselves grouped together almost by default.[7]

Jellyfish had at last found a home, albeit one without many strong determining characteristics. Once again, it was left to a relatively unknown French naturalist, this time François Péron, to draw attention to the scientific neglect that jellyfish were suffering from and which he claimed was due to 'the displeasure caused . . . as a result of their comical shapes, difficulties in description, illustration and preservation, and the fact they were disagreeable to touch, soft in composition and would decompose rapidly out of water.'[8]

Péron, who had been a soldier in the French Revolution and who trained subsequently in the art of dissection, had joined a scientific expedition to the southern hemisphere, sponsored by Emperor Napoleon, in 1800. The trip was beset with problems from the start. Despite its being the largest team of scientists ever to have set out on an expedition to explore the hypothetical continent 'Terra Australis', many jumped ship, others died of poor nutrition and scurvy, and of the 24 who set out on the voyage, only six returned alive. One was Péron, who survived just six more years before dying of tuberculosis. He made detailed observations of several different sorts of jellyfish and pointed to certain common features, again their radial symmetry, but also their unsegmented bodies, their lack of a head and their seemingly undifferentiated bodies. He also noted the relationship between weather patterns and jellyfish migrations and wrote a monograph on jellyfish illustrated by Charles-Alexandre Lésueur, published posthumously in 1809.

Following on from this, a German naturalist, Christian Ehrenberg, made a more detailed study of the jellyfish body and concluded that it was far more complex than it appeared at first sight. In a paper read to the Berlin Royal Academy in 1835 he

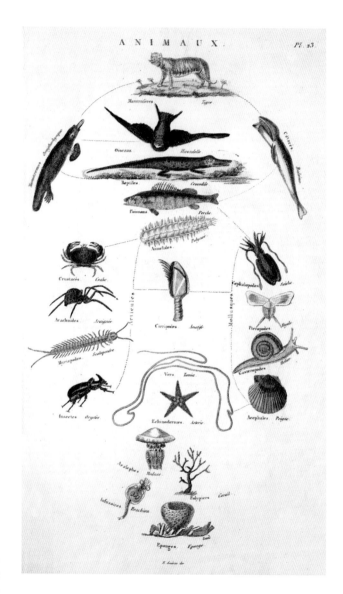

An example of
taxonomy before
Darwin. The
jellyfish come
low down in
the hierarchy
of animals.

The larva or 'ephyra' of a scyphozoan jellyfish.

indicated that, instead of being composed of an amorphous gelatinous material, the jellyfish had within its structure a highly organized arrangement of membranes and tiny vessels.[9] He was also able to confirm the presence of a digestive system with excretory pores, true muscle fibres, possible nerves and even eyes. No longer could the jellyfish be considered a simple, amorphous animal with little internal structure.

That hidden complexity was not just at an anatomical level. Jellyfish proved to have a complicated life history as well. This was revealed by a young Norwegian pastor with a passion for natural history called Michael Sars. In the 1830s he witnessed how a tiny jellyfish, merely a disc with deep lobes cut in it, detached itself from a stack of similar discs. The stack, or 'polyp', was sessile, in other words attached to a solid surface, while the small jellyfish that was budded off was free to move through the water. What Sars had witnessed was the asexual phase of reproduction in the

A jellyfish life cycle showing alternation of generations between sexual and asexual phases.

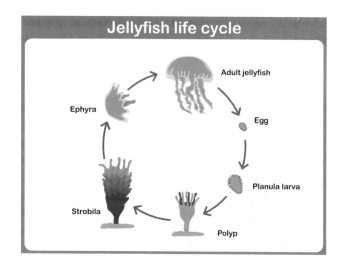

jellyfish in which a polyp would bud off small, immature medusae or ephyrae. These ephyrae, on maturing, then went through a sexual phase in which they either shed sperm or eggs into the sea, depending whether they were male or female. On being fertilized, the eggs turned into tiny larvae, or 'planulae', and these, after a free-swimming interval, settled on some solid surface, turning themselves back into polyps, the stacks that Sars had originally observed. What had been revealed was an 'alternation of generations' in jellyfish, a cycle in which asexual reproduction alternated with sexual reproduction in the same individual.[10]

The question arose: did the polyp come first, or was it the medusa? Further study showed that some species of jellyfish such as the mauve stinger, *Pelagia noctiluca*, lacked a polyp phase in their development, while others like the helmet jellyfish, *Periphylla periphylla*, appeared to have lost three stages: the planula, the polyp and the ephyra. There was even a small subset of jellyfish where the medusa itself was greatly reduced. Suddenly, the life history of jellyfish medusae and their polyp precursors became of interest to a wide group of scientists. For the general public, however, the medusa alone stood as the only recognizable representative of the group known as jellyfish.

If Cuvier provided the starting point for understanding animals in terms of their body plan, in the era that followed, some of the most influential zoologists applied their minds to relationships within the Radiata. Among them was a pupil of Cuvier, Louis Agassiz, who became interested in jellyfish after making his name as a scientist studying fossil fish. As Mary Winsor points out, there was a fundamental difference between Cuvier and Agassiz when it came to understanding animal structure. Cuvier believed structure was shaped by physiological necessity while Agassiz saw it as evidence of the hand of the Divine.[11] Agassiz's creationist views, at a time when Darwin held centre stage, brought him into conflict with many in the scientific world. Just as Darwin had made barnacles his own, so Agassiz made the study of different jellyfish his focus. He and his team of students would wade out into the coastal waters of New England in search of live specimens and, using his great powers of observation, he would teach his students the importance of looking and touching rather than simply reading and speculating about the jellyfish they encountered. How many got stung isn't recorded. His *Contributions to the Natural History of the United States of America*, published between 1857 and 1862, was largely devoted to these creatures and it is to Agassiz that we owe one of the best descriptions of the lion's mane jellyfish, *Cyanea capillata*:

seen floating in the water, it exhibits a large, circular disk of a substance not unlike jelly, thick in the centre and suddenly thinning out towards the edge, which presents several indentations. The centre of the disk is much lighter, almost white and transparent. The disk is constantly heaving and falling at regular intervals . . . From the lower surface of this disk hang conspicuously three kinds of appendages. Near the margin, there are eight bunches of long tentacles which can be compared to floating tresses of hair . . . alternating with these are eight bunches, four of which are elegant sacks adorned with waving ruffles . . . and four masses of folds hanging like rich curtains, loosely waving to and fro.[12]

Agassiz's biographer, Christoph Irmscher, said of him that he was to Darwin and his followers like one of his own jellyfish: 'weird, infinitely interesting, capable of inflicting a certain amount of harm, but ultimately destined to fade into insubstantiality'.[13]

It is certainly true that Agassiz had the power to attract and repel people in equal measure. One of the most charismatic teachers of his time, he spawned a generation of scientists and managed to accumulate a huge collection of zoological specimens that formed the basis of Harvard's Museum of Comparative Zoology. Yet his firm adherence to creationist ideas, combined with a belief in white supremacy, alienated many others.

While it was Agassiz who was responsible for recognizing the presence of a simple nervous system in jellyfish, it was two brothers, Oskar and Richard Hertwig, who developed this further.[14] Their collaborative work showed that ganglion cells existed in the inner and outer layers of the jellyfish and that processes from these cells formed a nerve net, or 'plexus', which connected to muscle cells. Through this arrangement, sensory information from the outside world was fed to the ganglion cells, which passed it on to muscle fibres, which in turn were able to respond by contracting. Their studies were to prove significant in understanding both primitive nervous systems, like that of a jellyfish, and how nervous systems developed in other animals. Sadly, their collaborative relationship dwindled with the passage of time. Not only were they very different personalities but they held opposing views on Darwinism. Oskar continued his scientific studies in Berlin while Richard moved to Munich.

Around the time that Agassiz was making his observations on jellyfish in America, another larger-than-life figure, Thomas Henry Huxley, was on the frigate *Rattlesnake* dissecting and making notes on the jellyfishes that could be retrieved from the water. The ship was on a mission to survey Australia's Great Barrier Reef as well as the seas around New Guinea. Huxley was an assistant surgeon on board ship and his skill in dissection helped him to discover the two-layered construction of the jellyfish body, composed of what he termed 'the foundation membranes', and to understand the significance of their stinging cells, now regarded as characteristic of cnidarian jellyfish. The product of his observations was a paper, 'On the Anatomy and the Affinities of the Family of the Medusae', which was sent initially to the bishop of Norwich (who was the father of the commander of the *Rattlesnake*), who, in turn, communicated it to the Royal Society.[15] So impressed with his piece of research were they that they awarded Huxley their Gold Medal. Later, Huxley was to become an energetic and vocal supporter of Darwin, so much so that he was given the title 'Darwin's bulldog'.

A few years later, another prominent personality of the time, Ernst Haeckel, made his own contribution to the story of jellyfish. He was one of a number of scientists who worked on the categorization of the material brought back from the *Challenger* expedition that had circumnavigated the globe.[16] His report on siphonophores (a particular type of colonial jellyfish which will be discussed in more depth in a later chapter), collected between 1873 and 1876, stretched to 380 pages, though his treatment of the group proved to be somewhat muddled. Between 1899 and 1904 Haeckel made a series of prints from the material he had collected, both siphonophores and other jellyfish medusae. These were later to be contained in a book, *Kunstformen der Natur*, one that was to prove highly influential in bridging the gap between art and science. Haeckel himself was an important marine biologist but some of the theories he propounded, such as the inheritance of acquired characteristics and his belief that the development of an animal expresses all the intermediate forms of its ancestors throughout evolution, proved to be incorrect. Like Agassiz, he was a good communicator with a strong following among his pupils.

Much of the groundwork in working out the structure and broad categories of jellyfish had been done by the end of the

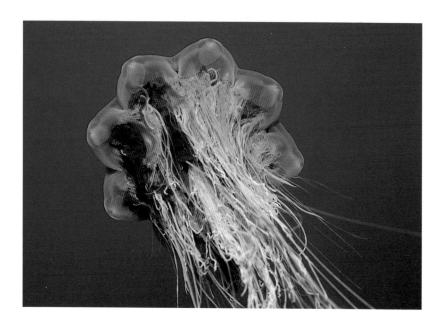

Lion's mane jellyfish, *Cyanea capillata*, one of the largest species of jellyfish.

A plate from Ernst Haeckel's *Kunstformen der Natur* (1904), illustrating the radial symmetry of medusa.

nineteenth century. What followed in jellyfish research amounted to a change of direction, much of it laboratory based. One of the first researchers to make direct observations of jellyfish in captivity, using plunger jars, was Marie Lebour (1876–1971) at Plymouth. She kept a diary of different medusae capturing, immobilizing and digesting their prey. Sometimes the process would take a few minutes, at other times over half an hour. She would illustrate the process with line drawings and noted how a jellyfish would dramatically increase its size over a relatively short period of time. Supplementing her observations by analysing the stomach contents of various planktonic animals caught in tow-nets, she provided crucial knowledge of the links in the food chain connecting jellyfish to different members of the plankton community. She also discovered that the moon jellyfish,

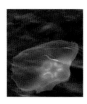

The moon jellyfish, *Aurelia aurita*, looking ethereal in the water.

Aurelia aurita, feeds on young fish when a juvenile but changes to a diet of small plankton such as copepod crustaceans and crab larvae when it reaches adulthood.[17]

While acknowledging the contribution made in understanding jellyfish in controlled environments like the laboratory, marine biologist Steven Haddock from Monterey put in a plea for examining the part they played, alongside other gelatinous zooplankton in the ecology of the oceans:

> Now, at the turn of the [twenty-first] century we have the opportunity to bring 'Gelata' [gelatinous creatures like jellyfish] back into primacy. Submersibles and remotely operated vehicles allow us to study entire life histories that we did not even know existed. The tools of molecular biology allow us to answer questions about development, evolution and phylogeny that had reached a stalemate. The critical roles these organisms play in the health of the oceans, their position at the crux of many evolutionary debates and the tools for biotechnology that they provide have led to a resurgent public appreciation and awareness [of these creatures].[18]

There is a long way to go before we properly understand the exact role jellyfish play in the ocean's ecology and how they evolved into such diverse groups. One thing is certain, however. Jellyfish remain enigmatic creatures, an attribution that has dominated their history from the start and one that shows a distinct reluctance to disappear. As one cultural historian, Celeste Olalquiaga, puts it:

> The jellyfish has an uncanny ability to seem what it is not; it is an animal that passes as a plant, a sort of natural

Mythical creatures. The mermaid finds shelter among the tentacles of a jellyfish.

transvestite. Beautiful to watch yet abrasive – even fatal – to touch, sheer and opaque, capable of continuous mutations, jellyfish have often been compared to those other mysterious creatures, women, who keep men guessing.[19]

2 Toxic but Fascinating

Contact with jellyfish is usually limited to an encounter with a dead specimen stranded on the shoreline, looking shapeless out of its watery environment. Occasionally it arises while swimming, when tentacles armed with stinging cells make contact with skin, causing a painful weal or an unpleasant rash. Either way, the encounter doesn't endear us to the animal. One collective noun for jellyfish is a 'smack', which encapsulates both the pain that is inflicted and the element of surprise this animal can produce when it makes contact.

There is another feature that stands in the way of endearment. That is its ability to produce mucus. Slime originates from cells in both the outer and inner layers of its body. There is understandably a reluctance to handle a jellyfish which goes beyond its propensity to sting. It is better viewed from a distance, preferably on a television screen, behind glass or as an illustration in a book. When jellyfish do appear in captivity, and then in specially designed tanks, they appear remote, ethereal and otherworldly. From the safety of the glass barrier we can begin to recognize their beauty and fragility, but there is still a long way to go before we form an attachment to the animal itself. Significantly, there is a paucity of soft toys in the shape of jellyfish; octopuses, yes (a few with fewer than eight tentacles!), but sadly very, very few jellyfish.

There is also something alien about the jellyfish, and it should come as no surprise that the animal served as the inspiration for the alien monsters in Steven Spielberg's film *War of the Worlds*. The creatures he devised had tank-like bodies and thin, flexible legs. Spielberg envisioned them as 'scary ballet dancers' and wanted them to dwarf humans, just as they did in H. G. Wells's original story.[1] No attempt was made at communication between these alien jellyfish and humans. Their intention to harm was made only too clear. Not so in the much praised sci-fi film *Arrival* directed by Denis Villeneuve.[2] Here the aliens that invaded the earth were again jellyfish-like; they had seven tentacles and were called 'heptapods', and their intentions were far less clear. They appeared not to understand humans and in turn we had difficulty understanding them. This barrier to comprehending each other's position was potent in causing fear. The film could be said to concern the role played by language in forging trust and

A 'tripod' from Spielberg's *War of the Worlds* (2005), showing its alien, jellyfish-like nature.

eradicating fear. The heptapods sought to communicate using a low-pitched thrum and inky, circular symbols. A professor of linguistics was recruited to decipher the language they were using, and in the end the aliens turned out to have benign intentions towards mankind.

Leading scientist Dr Maggie Aderin-Pocock, who works for the European space company Astrium, has even suggested that, instead of resembling little green men, aliens from outer space could look like jellyfish.[3] The picture she paints is of large, saucer-like creatures with buoyancy bags, imbibing chemical nutrients as they pass through clouds of methane and communicating by

Maggie Aderin-Pocock's vision of what aliens could look like. The idea that they might resemble humans, she believes, is wrong; more likely is that they resemble floating jellyfish.

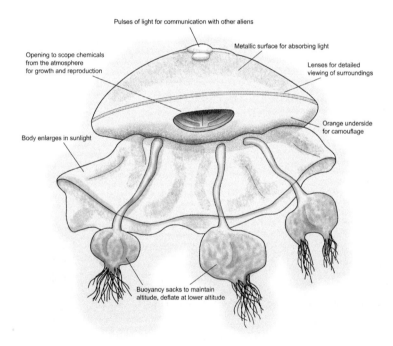

Pulses of light for communication with other aliens

Metallic surface for absorbing light

Opening to scope chemicals from the atmosphere for growth and reproduction

Lenses for detailed viewing of surroundings

Orange underside for camouflage

Body enlarges in sunlight

Buoyancy sacks to maintain altitude, deflate at lower altitude

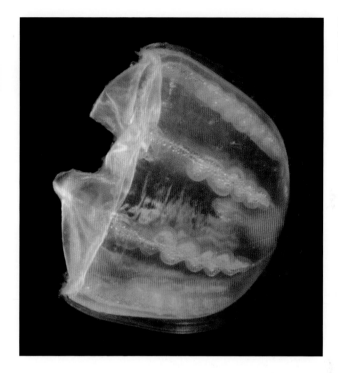

Deep sea jellyfish of the genus *Crossota*, described as alien-like.

means of pulses of light. Fanciful perhaps, but whenever a new species of jellyfish is discovered, usually living in the inky depths of the ocean, it is invariably described as an alien creature, not something belonging to this planet and planted there to confuse us. It is this otherworldly quality that arouses a suspicious, often hostile, response in us.

The harm and pain inflicted by a jellyfish can be significant. Those unfortunate enough to have been stung will know the intensity of the pain as well as the feeling of panic it can bring. A friend of mine described how, while swimming far out from the shore, he felt the unmistakable sting of not one but several jellyfish. He

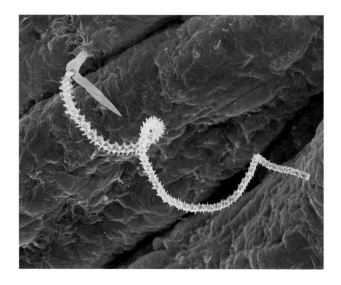

A discharged nematocyst of a box jellyfish viewed with a scanning electron microscope.

consciously executed fewer movements of his limbs in the water since bigger excursions might mean more contact with the 'enemy'. Reaching the shore, he was doused with iodine with no obvious immediate effect. Fortunately, his pain did slowly resolve. It had been a frightening experience. Likewise, the endurance swimmer Lewis Pugh had to put up with repeated jellyfish stings when he swam the entire length of the English Channel in 2018.

Jellyfish are the oldest extant lineage of venomous animals that are capable of subduing prey more recently evolved than themselves.[4] Central to their success is a reliance on stinging cells to capture and immobilize their prey. Each stinging cell, or nematocyst, houses a long, coiled, hollow tube which, on being stimulated, everts itself with great force at an estimated velocity of 2 m (6.5 ft) per second. The tube itself is often armed with barbs and through it passes a cocktail of chemicals able to initiate both toxic and immunological reactions in its prey. The venom has a complex composition containing enzymes that break down tissues, neurotoxins that excite nerves, as well as pore-forming toxins that cause cells to leak their contents. In addition, the venom induces the release of chemicals in its victim which augments the toxic effect. So-called 'penetrant nematocysts' are a feature of all jellyfish belonging to the phylum Cnidaria and are found mostly on the tentacles and around the mouth and oral arms, as well as occasionally on the bell. What precisely causes the nematocyst to discharge its lethal thread is incompletely understood. It is believed that mechanical and chemical factors are involved and that, once discharged, the cell is rendered useless and has to be replaced. Prey such as fish, shrimps, eggs and larvae of different sorts, and even other jellyfish, are subdued by the sting and passed to the mouth by the tentacles and then broken down and digested internally. In humans, the effects of a jellyfish sting can vary in severity from the mildly irritant to the life threatening, depending on the exact species of animal and the size of the imprint on the skin left by the tentacles. Though temporary discomfort and a mark on the skin is the usual result of contact with a tentacle, sometimes the outcome is substantially worse.

Weals as the result of contact with a box jellyfish.

Sign warning about the dangers of Portuguese men-of-war, *Physalia physalis*, on Queensland beach, 2017.

Wearing a 'stinger suit' does offer protection. These are usually made of nylon or spandex and are light to wear and keep their shape. However, if contact occurs with even a small area of bare skin an unpleasant reaction is possible. Current advice for treating jellyfish stings is far from consistent. Pouring cold water over the affected area can cause further release of the venom from adherent tentacles and is best avoided, while the widely held notion that urine relieves the pain, as popularized in the sitcom *Friends*, is a myth. Sometimes applying vinegar helps and bottles of it can be seen on beaches along the coast of Queensland. Attempts to detach tentacles from the victim's skin risk massive discharge from the stinging cells so isn't generally recommended. Considerable effort is being expended now in understanding how better to treat jellyfish stings and in knowing more about the differences between jellyfish types in terms of their venom. Experts in the field of venom research, such Bryan Fry at the University of Queensland, admit that progress is slow. Not only can there be problems in extracting sufficient venom from individual jellyfish, but the molecular chemistry is complex and differs in different jellyfish.[5]

Back in the early 1930s a connection was established between an acute illness characterized by severe headache, backache, nausea, sweating and a profound feeling of anxiety and the act of being stung while swimming off the coast of Queensland. The features of this syndrome were investigated by a doctor called Hugo Flecker but the identity of the stinging object remained elusive. He gave the syndrome the name 'Irukandji' after a local aboriginal tribe. Following his death in 1957, another doctor, Jack Barnes, continued Flecker's work. He suspected the cause of the syndrome might be a particular species of jellyfish. Noting the locations where the 'illness' had struck, Barnes concluded the offending agent was likely to be small and transparent. This would explain why it had gone unnoticed for so long. Because episodes tended to cluster over time, it was thought likely that the causative agent only appeared episodically and then in significant numbers. Following a report of several cases of the Irukandji syndrome on a particular stretch of coastline, Barnes was able to identify a possible culprit, a particular jellyfish, and to prove the link he tested the sting of this creature on himself as well as on his nine-year-old son. Both reported excruciating pain as well as other features consistent with the syndrome. Thankfully, both survived and the box jellyfish responsible was named *Carukia barnesi* in honour of its discoverer.[6] Dr Barnes was however unsuccessful in finding an antidote to the sting but found that wearing women's tights in the water was effective in preventing jellyfish from causing harm. It would seem that stinging cells were normally triggered to release their poison by chemicals on the skin of its prey but were not stimulated when in contact with the material used in the tights.

It was in 1752 that Linnaeus gave jellyfish the alternative name 'medusa' from the Greek myth of the same name. The term was well chosen. The bell of a jellyfish is a reminder of the head of the Gorgon sister, with its tentacles, like snakes, substituting for hair. Both the mythical Medusa and her animal counterpart were capable of causing paralysis and even death. In the version of the Medusa myth found in Ovid's *Metamorphoses*, Medusa, one of three Gorgon sisters, was originally depicted as a great beauty whose attractive powers did not go unnoticed.[7] Her hair was only transformed into serpents by the goddess Athena as a punishment. Medusa had been ravished by the sea god Poseidon in Athena's own temple and because the temple had been defiled, Athena gave Medusa the power to change any human who looked upon her into stone. Perseus, the son of Zeus and half-brother of Athena, was asked by Polydectes to secure the head of Medusa. Instead of gazing on the Gorgon sister and risking being petrified, Perseus used the reflection on his shield to guide him while removing Medusa's head with his sword. From her decapitated torso sprang two children, Pegasus, a flying horse, and Chrysaor, a warrior with a golden sword. The transformative powers of Medusa's head were retained following its separation from the body and when Perseus laid down the head on the seashore, the escaping blood was said to be the origin of red coral (intriguing, knowing the close relationship that exists between jellyfish and coral).

Caravaggio's depiction of Medusa, painted towards the end of the sixteenth century, echoes her destructive yet beautiful power while another painting, initially thought to be by Leonardo da Vinci, was to inspire a famous poem by Shelley:

'Tis the tempestuous loveliness of terror;
For from the serpents gleams a brazen glare

One of two versions of Caravaggio's *Medusa*, c. 1597, oil on canvas on wooden shield.

Kindled by that inextricable error,
Which makes a thrilling vapour of the air
Become a [ ] and ever-shifting mirror.
Of all the beauty and the terror there-
A woman's countenance, with serpent locks,
Gazing in death on heaven from those wet rocks.[8]

A more up-to-date version of Medusa is seen in Frank Moore's painting *To Die For*. It features the model Kate Moss, her severed head alive with serpents. It was a painting commissioned by Gianni Versace, who never saw it since he was killed before Moore had completed the work. Moore himself died prematurely of AIDS

A modern-day Medusa. Frank Moore, *To Die For*, 1997, oil on canvas on featherboard with mirror frame.

in 2002, aged 48. The picture featured in an exhibition in New York called *Toxic Beauty: The Art of Frank Moore*.[9]

In her poem 'Medusa', Sylvia Plath successfully combines the mythical creature and the sea animal.[10] Written shortly before her own death, it portrays her mother, with whom she had a difficult relationship, as a destructive monster clinging to her by a 'cable', akin to a jellyfish tentacle, and intent on controlling, indeed paralysing, her. It is as though Plath felt the need to exorcize her mother from her life in order to achieve some emotional distance, as well as to afford her greater freedom to write and compose. Plath could be said to have used the device of the snake-haired Gorgon to describe her own internal image of a monstrous mother. Ironically, her mother shared her first name with that of a common genus of jellyfish, *Aurelia*.

Freud came to regard Medusa's head as a symbol of castration. In a short, posthumously published essay, 'Das Medusenhaupt',[11] he equates decapitation with being castrated, arguing that when a boy views female genitalia for the first time he suddenly realizes the possession of a penis cannot be taken for granted, leading to a specific anxiety about castration. In the same way, glimpsing the Medusa's head causes a male observer to be struck dumb, on the one hand fascinated by what he sees and, on the other, paralysed with fear.

The Medusa myth, with its built-in ambiguity (deadly but fascinating), has served to reinforce our own ambivalence towards this sea creature. It may also have created a reluctance on the part of scientists to work with these animals. There is however no doubting that, when seen in its natural environment, the jellyfish displays that other, more positive quality, an ability to hold our attention, indeed to fascinate. This is explored in Marianne Moore's poem 'A Jelly-fish', where the creature exerts 'a fluctuating charm'.[12]

Jellyfish escape as quickly as they appear and while they may be allowed to touch us, they themselves often resist capture. They appear both alluring and elusive. The very nature of their movement contributes to their ethereal beauty, and where better to observe this than in a tropical lagoon? The Raja Ampat islands off West Papua boast several. Others can be found on the Kakaban islands off Borneo. In both places the jellyfish have lost their ability to sting humans, making it possible to appreciate their delicacy and movement in safety. In the Ampat islands, the lagoons are connected to the ocean through underwater channels that limit the entry and exit of seawater. In addition, the water there is stratified into an oxygen-rich surface layer where the jellyfish live and a deeper layer, devoid of oxygen, where they are absent. Two genera of jellyfish, the so-called golden jellyfish, *Mastigias*, and the moon jellyfish, *Aurelia*, coexist there. The species of *Mastigias* found in Ampat has lost the spots on its bell and oral arms and the marine biologist Michael Dawson believes this indicates a new subspecies has evolved there with no appreciable sting, presumably as the result of geographical isolation.[13]

The slow, seemingly directionless pulsation of jellyfish can have a calming effect and lends itself to hospital and general

practice waiting rooms, a feature as yet unexploited. Its languid movement calls into question how efficient this is as a means of locomotion. Work done at Woods Hole Marine Biological Laboratory in Massachusetts is providing the answer. It seems that jellyfish have a special way of recapturing some of the energy expended on each swimming stroke. When a medusa contracts its bell, it creates two vortex rings. The first is shed in its wake, propelling the animal forwards. The second, during the relaxation phase, rolls under the bell. This second vortex ring spins faster than the first and, as it does so, sucks in water which pushes up against the underside of the bell, giving the jellyfish a secondary boost. It is a technique that works only at slow speeds and when the body size is small. The conclusion reached by Brad Gemmell and his team at Woods Hole is that a jellyfish expends less energy in travelling a given distance than any other marine

Snorkelling in Jellyfish Lake, Palau.

The golden jellyfish, *Mastigias*, from Jellyfish Lake, Palau.

Festo 'Air Jelly', 2008. The first indoor flying object with peristaltic propulsion inspired by a jellyfish.

animal so far studied. Its efficiency, however, comes at a price, namely low speed and virtually no manoeuvrability.[14]

It would be wrong, however, to dismiss the humble jellyfish as a primitive automaton, unable to modify its movement and behaviour. By attaching accelerometers to the barrel jellyfish, *Rhizostoma pulmo*, it has been shown that it is able to orientate its swimming in relation to the direction of the tides. When the tide withdraws from the shore, this particular jellyfish orientates itself so as to swim against the current. When the tide flows towards the shore, it also swims in a consistent direction, either with or against the current, depending on the depth of the water. This appears to be a mechanism for keeping jellyfish together as a swarm and avoiding their becoming stranded on the shore.[15]

The fascination that jellyfish engender in us deepens when we consider recent discoveries about another aspect of their behaviour, one which mirrors our own. In the so-called upside-down jellyfish, *Cassiopea*, it is possible to witness periods of diminished activity resembling sleep from which the creature is only slowly aroused (reminiscent of our own behaviour when

Barrel jellyfish, *Rhizostoma plumo*, thought to be capable of orientating itself to the prevailing tide.

50

The upside-down jellyfish, *Cassiopea andromeda*. Sometimes mistaken for a sea anemone, it can deliver a powerful sting. There are several coloured varieties.

sleep deprived).[16] Like us, this jellyfish becomes 'sleepy' when exposed to the naturally occurring chemical melatonin. Sleep, or at least periods of cyclical inactivity, would appear to have arisen early on in evolution, well in advance of the possession of advanced nervous systems.

Earlier in the book, I stressed how the anatomy and the life cycle of jellyfish proved to be more complex than previously imagined. The behaviour of jellyfish in their natural habitat is proving equally complicated. We know that migrations of jellyfish in a horizontal direction are guided by the position of the sun. The golden jellyfish in Palau, for example, follow the sun's arc across the sky. Before sunrise, they cluster at the western end of Jellyfish Lake. With the dawn, they swim in an easterly direction towards the light, following the sun until they reach the eastern shore. As the sun continues towards the western horizon, the jellyfish reverse their course and return to the western shore to await the new day.[17]

Vertical migration also occurs. Using echo sounders in a deep Norwegian fjord, the movements of individual helmet jellyfish, *Periphylla periphylla*, were monitored. This species of jellyfish segregates itself into assemblages. Each assemblage shows a different preference as far as vertical positioning in the water is concerned. Night-time groups congregate for the purpose of feeding and reproduction while other groups form for brief periods in other situations, only to disperse and then re-group. It has been suggested that this represents a type of social behaviour and raises the question of what cues they use to seek each other out. Jellyfish may not be the passive drifters we imagine after all. Acoustic studies combined with observations using submersibles and the use of electronic tagging may yet reveal more sophisticated patterns of behaviour.[18]

David Albert from the Roscoe Bay Marine Biological Laboratory in Vancouver goes so far as to declare jellyfish really do have a brain of sorts. Studying the moon jellyfish, *Aurelia*, he was able to confirm that they swam upwards in response to being touched by a predatory jellyfish, downwards in response to low salinity, and furthermore showed additional behaviours such as avoiding turbulence, forming aggregations in the water and exhibiting directional swimming in a horizontal plane. These responses appeared not to be simple reflexes but constituted an organized set of behaviours requiring sensory feedback for their execution. These numerous adaptive behaviours, he believes, have been critical to their survival.[19]

The gap that exists between 'us and them' may indeed be narrowing. As the author Robert Macfarlane points out, studying animals in the wild reminds us of worlds other than our own, worlds operating in ways and with purposes we fail to understand;[20] a good enough reason for continuing to study jellyfish in their natural environment.

3 Floats, Eyes and Combs

Diversity among jellyfish demands a chapter of its own, so great is the variety of shape, colour and micro-structure. As a student of zoology many years ago, I had to read the first volume of Libbie Henrietta Hyman's monumental work *The Invertebrates: Protozoa through Ctenophora*. I remember poring over the detailed drawings of jellyfish and thinking how absurdly different they all were, from ribbon-like creatures, to globular animals with appendages, to flattened, disc-like forms. It was as though there was little or no connection between them apart from their gelatinous composition and their planktonic way of life. Was it simply that jellyfish had been around for a very long time and so had more opportunities than other animals to diversify?

Purists will argue that only scyphozoans are 'true' jellyfish. This however ignores the fact that the term 'jellyfish' is used by the public in a much wider sense. The familiar jellyfish we see in coastal waters with its radially symmetrical bell and tentacles falling like curtains around its edge is the scyphomedusa. Similar to it, but with a bell flattened on four sides and tentacles only in the corners, is the cubomedusa, or box jellyfish, while another cousin, within the same phylum, Cnidaria, is the hydromedusa, which tends to be smaller than the scyphomedusa but has within its group larger colonial forms whose body plan is entirely different. Most scyphozoans, several hydrozoans and all cubozoans alternate their life cycles between a sessile (fixed) polyp stage and a pelagic (drifting) medusa stage, as was described in the last chapter. Some hydrozoans, on the other hand, are composed of modified medusoid and polyploid individuals living together as a single unit. These are known as siphonophores. To complete the picture, there is a fourth group, the ctenophores or comb jellies, which at one time were included within the Cnidaria in a grouping known as the Coelenterata. All of them possessed a body cavity, or coelenteron, had a two-layered body wall construction and a gelatinous composition and were either transparent or translucent. However, ctenophores lacked the stinging cells which typified the cnidarian jellyfish and possessed other complex bodily structures not found anywhere else. A separate designation for ctenophores beckoned and, before long, they were placed in a phylum of their own.

It is worth emphasizing how incomplete our knowledge of all these gelatinous sea creatures is. New species of jellyfish are constantly being discovered, often deep in the oceans or under ice caps. Better sampling techniques allow complete, rather than fragmented, specimens to be examined. Also, improvements in underwater photography have made it possible to film those that inhabit the ocean depths where no light penetrates. Most found in deep water are proving to be new to science, emphasizing how much remains to be discovered. Their number and significance as components of the food web is only now being appreciated. Most are predatory in their habits, though they could best be described as fishermen rather than active hunters, trapping their prey as they do with stinging cells or sticky threads.

Until 1880 it was thought that all jellyfish lived in the sea. Then, much to everyone's amazement, an unmistakable jellyfish was found in a water tank containing a giant water lily in Regent's Park.[1] It was a freshwater hydromedusa and four years elapsed

The 'dandelion' siphonophore observed during an exploration of deep water by NOAA's *Okeanos Explorer*.

before its polyp stage was discovered. *Craspedacusta sowerbii*, as it came to be known, was subsequently found in other freshwater locations throughout the world, often in artificial bodies of water such as gravel pits or reservoirs. How they arrived at these locations isn't known, but it is possible they were transported there on the feet of birds. Specimens tended to be small in size and within one place their numbers would fluctuate considerably. Their sting could not be felt by humans, though they used nematocysts to capture prey, such as small crustaceans.

Within the phylum Cnidaria, it is the hydrozoans that display most diversity of form, having both solitary and colonial forms. One order in particular has attracted a lot of attention from the moment it was first discovered: the siphonophores. Bearing scant resemblance to other jellyfish, they lack the radial symmetry typical of the group and instead are composed of numerous sacs, feelers, shields and tentacles, joined together in a bewildering way. They posed a considerable challenge to early taxonomists who had to invent new terms to describe the features they saw. Most were small and fragile but some, like the Portuguese man-of-war, *Physalia physalis*, were large and floated on the surface of the sea. Each Portuguese man-of-war had a gas-filled float, the pneumatophore, which would sit above the water surface with a sail to catch the wind. Beneath hung different, yet genetically identical, individuals called zooids, each of which performed a specific task. Some would capture prey (dactylozooids), others were responsible for feeding the colony (gastrozooids) and yet more were involved in reproduction (gonozooids). *Physalia* wasn't simply a collection of discrete organisms but an integrated whole in which each zooid depended for its existence on the others. Its distinctive structure raised the question as to whether it was an individual in its own right or a colony of individuals. This precise

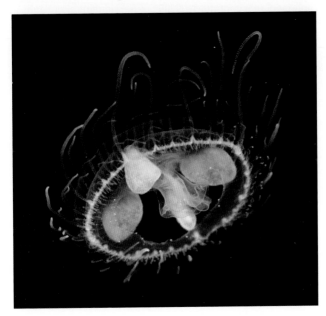

The fresh-water jellyfish, *Craspedacusta sowerbii*, first recorded in England in 1880. Populations found tend to be either all male or all female.

issue was to ignite an important debate in the nineteenth century between T. H. Huxley, Louis Agassiz and Ernst Haeckel, three major players in the field of jellyfish research whose names were mentioned earlier.

Huxley held the view that Portuguese men-of-war were individual organisms and their respective parts were organs. He quoted this example in an essay on the nature of individuality in biology.[2] Agassiz, on the other hand, saw them as colonies, while Haeckel, who was responsible for describing the siphonophores collected during the voyage of the *Challenger*, held the middle ground, claiming they were in part colonies and in part organisms. The question as to whether siphonophores were organisms or colonies later inspired Stephen Jay Gould to write, 'both and neither; they lie in the middle of a continuum where one grades into the other'.[3] Siphonophores continue to challenge our thinking about animal organization. As one emeritus professor put it, 'Siphonophores

A Portuguese man-of-war, *Physalia physalis*, showing its mohawk-like pneumatophore. The gas within it has a higher concentration of carbon monoxide than the surrounding air.

have reached the organ grade of construction by converting whole individuals into organs'.[4]

Today the term 'cormidium' is used to describe the parts of a siphonophore that act together and which are physically joined to one another along a main stem. As the colony grows, so new cormidia are added. To make sense of siphonophore anatomy, it is perhaps easiest to divide the colony into two functional parts: an upper part or nectosome, and a lower part or siphostome. The nectosome bears a number of swimming bells, above which is often a small float. The bells can be replaced by budding new ones off from beneath the float. The stem below, or siphostome, bears the cormidia with their distinct zooids, each one performing a separate function. This basic plan is however subject to considerable variation.

Praya dubia or giant siphonophore, the second longest sea creature after the bootlace worm.

Siphonophore life histories are as varied as their anatomy and only incompletely understood.[5] One of the longest animals in the world, *Praya dubia*, happens to be a siphonophore. It can grow to 50 m (164 ft) in length and inhabits a world of darkness. Living deep in the ocean, it experiences high external water pressures. Bringing the animal up to the water surface causes its elements to explode, but in its own environment it alternates between being motionless and being actively mobile. Movement is brought about by contracting its swimming bells, which act as jets. During this moving phase, its tentacles are retracted. In its motionless phase, a blue luminescence emitted by this jellyfish attracts prey which become trapped in a curtain of tentacles. Another much smaller siphonophore, *Muggiaea atlantica*, is able to swim in a spiral manner and its motion has been likened to that of a bullfighter in the ring. Mostly, however, siphonophores drift passively in the water at the mercy of winds and currents and, like 'true' jellyfish, are unable to actively pursue their prey. The sting their tentacles deliver can be a powerful disincentive to other predators, though

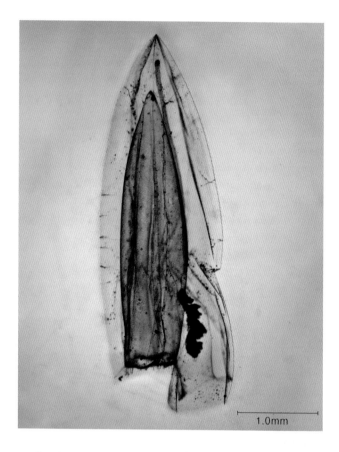

Muggiaea atlantica, a small siphonophore jellyfish, held responsible for the death of farmed salmon in Norway.

1.0mm

sand crabs are able to make a meal out of a stranded Portuguese man-of-war and some sea slugs, like the blue dragon, *Glaucus atlanticus*, are able to eat siphonophores and even incorporate their stinging cells into their own feathery appendages as weapons. As a consequence, it doesn't pay to pick up a blue dragon.

An interesting association occurs between the Portuguese man-of-war and a certain species of fish. The bluebottle fish, *Nomeus gronovii*, feeds on the jellyfish's tentacles but manages to avoid the zooids that contain the stinging cells. It would appear that the jellyfish benefits from this arrangement since the presence of a live fish among its tentacles acts as a lure to attract other fish on which it feeds. Some deep-sea siphonophores, like *Erenna*, have extensions to their bodies in the form of lures which actively attract prey. These can glow red and twitch in ways that mimic the jerky movements of the tiny crustacea on which this jellyfish feeds. As their discoverers point out, they are the first-known invertebrates able to make red light and the first non-visual predators to use luminescent lures.[6] There seems no end to the bizarre adaptations found in deep-sea siphonophores; the problem lies in accessing these unusual jellyfish. Some of what is known about siphonophores is the result of work done at Villefranche-sur-Mer on the French Riviera. There, siphonophores normally found in deep sea can be found in surface waters, making Villefranche a convenient sampling point.

Blue dragon sea-slug, *Glaucus atlanticus*, consuming a Portuguese man-of-war.

On this stamp the bluebottle fish, *Nomeus gronovii*, takes shelter among the tentacles of a Portuguese man-of-war.

Tentilla of the siphonophore *Erenna* and, among them, red luminescent lures to attract prey.

While a siphonophore's sting can be unpleasant, that of a box jellyfish can be lethal. The most venomous of all species, *Chironex fleckeri*, is responsible for the loss of several lives each year in Australia and East Asia. It is a sizeable jellyfish with tentacles up to 2 m (6–7 ft) in length. *Carukia barnesi*, previously mentioned in connection with Irukandji syndrome, is much more difficult to see, being transparent and only the size of a thumbnail. Jamie Seymour at James Cook University in Australia leads one of the main research groups looking at box jellyfish ecology and the treatment of its stings. His main focus is on their breeding behaviour, since early detection of these jellyfish may save lives and so benefit the tourist industry on Australia's beaches, which continues to suffer during the box jellyfish season. He expresses doubts as to whether the correct first aid is currently being given in the event of a sting.[7]

Another unusual and distinguishing feature of the box jellyfish is its fast, directional movement in the water. Some can achieve speeds of 2 m per second. Pulsation of the bell, which has a narrow aperture, creates a powerful water jet. The animal's movement through the water is guided by complex visual equipment.[8] On each of the four sides of the box jellyfish is a sensory club, or rhopalium, which over time has evolved into a cluster of eyes,

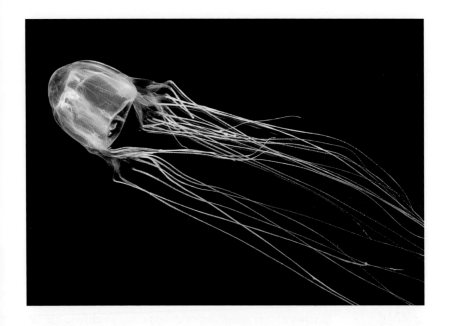

some even resembling our own. They are of three types: two have spherical lenses placed medially, two are pit eyes and two are slit eyes. The pit eyes have just one type of cell and act as light meters. The slit eyes are capable of spatial resolution along a single axis, while the eyes with lenses have a typical camera-like structure similar to our own with a hemispherical retina behind each lens. Each type of eye performs a specific function but they act together in concert to direct movement.

Yet more surprises are to be found among box jellyfish. As a result of observing a *Carybdea sivickisi* (also known as *Copula sivickisi*) in the laboratory, two researchers, Cheryl Lewis Ames and Tristan Long, showed that mature adults actually engage in courtship prior to mating, extraordinary when you consider they lack a central nervous system.[9] After approximating tentacles,

The box jellyfish, *Chironex fleckeri*, commonly known as the sea wasp.

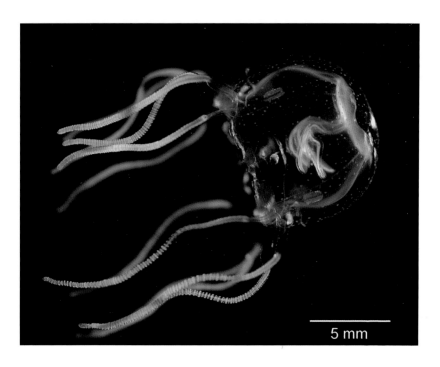

5 mm

The Caribbean box jellyfish, *Tripedalia cystophora*, showing rhopalia, each carrying a set of six eyes. With these they can successfully avoid obstacles.

packages containing sperm are transferred from the male to the female, who shows her maturity by displaying conspicuous markings on her bell margin. These packages are ingested, like food, through the mouth and then partially digested in the body cavity so that the sperm, or at least their nuclei, are released intact. These then find their way to the female gonads containing the eggs. Fertilization is therefore brought about internally (this in contrast to what happens in the majority of jellyfish, which simultaneously release sperm and eggs into the water, fertilization being therefore external). Sperm packages are received from several males by the same female and, somewhat surprisingly, stinging cells are included. Stinging cells are also to be found in the female gonads.

Some of these stinging cells are transferred to the new embryos, which are shed a few days later. They are believed to act as a deterrent to any predator seeking to eat the developing larvae.

In considering the structure of both box jellyfish and siphonophores, we have strayed a long way from Louis Agassiz's description of a lion's mane jellyfish, but scyphozoan jellyfish themselves can show several unusual features. The upside-down jellyfish *Cassiopea*, mentioned previously in connection with periods of inactivity, obtains most of its nutritional needs from algae that inhabit its body and which draw their energy from the sun. These algae are zooxanthellae and can be found occasionally in other members of the Cnidaria, such as corals and sea anemones. Another scyphozoan jellyfish, *Bazinga rieki*, which is the size of a grape, also uses zooxanthellae to manufacture food as a result of photosynthesis. It has no tentacles and pulsates at a disconcertingly rapid rate to keep its position in the water. The name 'bazinga' derives from a term meaning 'fooled you!', a colloquialism from the mouth of Dr Sheldon Cooper in the TV series *The Big Bang Theory*, and refers to the fact that it was mistaken for a juvenile of an existing species until examined by Lisa-ann Gershwin and Peter Davie in 2013.[10] A further example of a scyphozoan jellyfish, *Deepstaria enigmatica*, certainly lives up to its name.[11] It is one of the largest jellyfish predators and, though first described over 45 years ago, it has been encountered on very few occasions. It lives in deep water, has a thin, sheet-like body and lacks tentacles. Observations made by David Gruber, Brennan Phillips, Leigh Marsh and John Sparks using an imaging system mounted on a remotely operated vehicle have shown *Deepstaria* trapping its prey by enveloping it in its thin umbrella and then tightening its edge like a drawstring so nothing can escape. This bagging of its prey and the animal's peristaltic way of moving make it unique among scyphozoan jellyfish. It is also unusual in having a highly branched network of canals distributed over its umbrella, giving its surface a reticular appearance. A carcass of this jellyfish has been observed to provide food for crabs living on the ocean bottom. Such 'jelly falls' are thought to provide a significant source of food for those inhabiting the deep sea.

Mention has already been made of ctenophores, or comb jellies, and of how different they are from other jellyfish. Those who enjoy the seriously weird need look no further than these strange animals. Often referred to as 'the aliens of the sea', they possess combs made of iridescent cilia that propel them up and down columns of water. The word ctenophore (the 'c', as in Cnidaria, is silent) comes from the Greek meaning comb-bearer and they present a bewildering array of different shapes, from the spherical to the ribbon-like. First recorded by a ship's surgeon, Friderich Martens, in 1671 near Spitsbergen, they were found a century later in Jamaica by Patrick Brown. Just two species were included in Linnaeus' *Systema naturae*. We now recognize over two hundred species and that may be the tip of the iceberg. Not only are they numerous and possibly the least understood examples of jellyfish, but one species, *Mnemiopsis leidyi*, having been accidentally introduced into the Black Sea, managed to destroy the fishing industry there, causing havoc to the food chain, a story which is taken up in a later chapter.

The uniqueness of ctenophores lies in their many unusual features. The round ones are often represented in textbooks upside down because of a badly named apical organ which lies at the opposite pole to the mouth. It is a gravity sensor. While the mouth in a conventional medusa points down, in ctenophores it points up, in the direction of movement. Radiating from the apical organ are eight longitudinal rows of cilia that diffract light and display a rainbow-like hue. Up to the nineteenth century it was believed that, as with cnidarian jellyfish, a single aperture acted both as a mouth and an anus. It has since been shown that ctenophores have a through-gut, a mouth and, opposite it, small openings through which waste matter can be discharged. This discovery has caused scientists to rethink the evolution of the anus. Ctenophores exist at all levels in the sea but because of their fragility they are difficult to collect intact and study. Small wonder their ubiquity and diversity of form wasn't appreciated. They are predatory in their habits, feeding on zooplankton, including other jellyfish. Two contractile tentacles are normally present and attached to them are batteries of cells called collo-blasts which produce a sticky secretion used in capturing prey. So-called 'lobate' ctenophores have their own way of trapping prey – large, muscular surfaces covered in mucus. Members of the group known as beroids boast a large, flexible mouth that is used to devour prey much larger than them. Instead of having tentacles, they bite into other jellyfish using teeth. Perhaps the most interesting feature of all is the ctenophore nervous system. It takes the form of a nerve net with connections between nerves called synapses, analogous to the ones in our own nervous system. The difference between their synapses and ours is in the type of chemical, or neurotransmitter, that bridges the gap. This has caused scientists to reconsider the evolution of nervous systems in animals and to suggest that the use of neurotransmitters may have evolved independently on at least two occasions.[12]

Among all living animals, ctenophores comprise one of the least studied phyla. Their taxonomy is confused and, as Casey Dunn and others have pointed out, they are subject to several misconceptions. First, they are labelled as primitive when in fact they exhibit numerous complex and unique features. Second, while superficially resembling medusae, being transparent and gelatinous, they display many differences, not least an absence of stinging cells. Third is their symmetry. It is neither radial nor bilateral. Instead the halves have to be rotated through 180 degrees in order to achieve symmetry and this is known as rotational symmetry. Ctenophores hold a special place in the animal kingdom but, as Dunn points out, because their unusual features are not shared with other animals, they do not give us any clear idea of their relationship with other animals. They appear to have diverged early on in evolution, but that doesn't mean they resemble the most recent common ancestor. Fossil ctenophores have been found in southern Germany and owe their preservation to the rapid precipitation of pyrite in their tissues. More have been found in the famous Burgess Shale deposits in America. Whether

Deepstaria enigmatica, a rare and mysterious jellyfish resembling a plastic bag in the water and named after Jacques Cousteau's submersible, *Deepstaria 4000*.

The ctenophore known as the sea gooseberry, *Pleurobrachia pileus*, showing a pair of retractable tentacles fringed with filaments along one edge.

ctenophores or sponges represent the sister group of all other living animals is currently being debated. Most would agree that ctenophores are just different and weird.

So far, my aim has been to emphasize the immense diversity in form, structure and traits within the artificial grouping known as jellyfish. Three authorities, Casey Dunn, Sally Leys and Steven Haddock, make the point that while jellyfish have traditionally been regarded as 'lower' animals ('lower' in the sense that they are thought to embody several primitive features), this ignores the fact that they possess complex traits, ones that have been gained over time, just as others, doubtless, have been lost.[13] They include combs made of cilia, glue cells or 'colloblasts', a type of statocyst not found elsewhere and a body symmetry which is neither radial nor bilateral. These features, they argue, should make us resist calling them primitive, and while considerable progress has been made of late in understanding the relationships animals have to one another (for example, in defining the five 'clades' or groupings to which all animals belong), nevertheless we are at an early stage in our understanding of what features have been acquired and what lost in the course of evolution. The study of animal diversity can be potentially productive in understanding early animal evolution and, in this important area of study, jellyfish have a lot to offer.

4 The Illustrator's Nightmare

It is a matter of curiosity that while octopuses figure frequently on potters' jars in Minoan Crete and in mosaics from Roman times, jellyfish tend not to. Aboriginal rock and bark paintings do include jellyfish, but we have to wait until the sixteenth century before we have an accurate representation of a medusa. This comes from Conrad Gessner's *Historia animalium*, widely regarded as the first proper zoological treatise. Gessner, known as 'the German Pliny', was born far from the sea in Zurich, but travelled widely in Europe. In the abbreviated version of the book, *Icones animalium*, published in 1560, under the heading *Urtica* we see an unequivocal jellyfish.[1] Interestingly, in the book it is aligned with octopuses within a grouping called *Mollis*, or 'soft creatures'. Its tentacles appear stiff, but there is no doubt about which animal it is.

Ulisse Aldrovandi, a naturalist and a leading figure in the Italian Renaissance movement, has a better likeness of a medusa in his *Historia naturalis* of 1606, labelled *Pulmo marinus.* Aldrovandi had one of the most comprehensive cabinets of curiosities in Europe. An illustration in book four of *De Zoophytis* bears a strong likeness to a blubber jellyfish.[2] His network of naturalists and travellers saw to it that he was made aware of a wide variety of animals, some of them fanciful in the extreme; others, like jellyfish, were more immediately recognizable. As well as illustrating

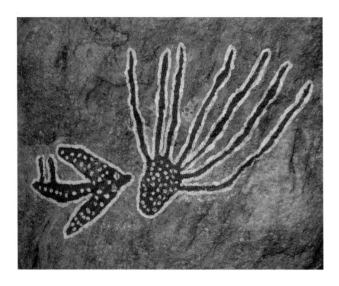

Aboriginal rock art showing a jellyfish from Bathurst Head, Queensland.

animal life, Aldrovandi was a great collector of natural objects and he became the first professor of natural sciences in Bologna.

Being friable, having neither an internal nor an external skeleton and with over 95 per cent of their body composed of water, meant that jellyfish were difficult to collect in one piece, to handle and to preserve. Because of this, early naturalists had to rely on illustrators to document their gross anatomy and record their colour and detail before the specimens under inspection disintegrated. Theirs was not an easy job. Charles-Alexandre Lésueur had to make sketches on board ship from damaged specimens, knowing the jellyfish in question would disappear in a short space of time. It is a wonder anything was depicted. Yet Lésueur, who became known as 'the Raphael of zoological painters', produced some astonishing work using the drawings of jellyfish he made on board ship to create watercolour paintings on vellum when he returned to France in 1804.[3] Lésueur had originally enlisted as an assistant gunner on board an expedition to Terra Australis led by Captain Nicolas Baudin. He only stepped into the role of illustrator when the three appointed artists on the expedition fell sick or abandoned ship. The corvette *Le Géographe* and its sister ship *Le Naturaliste* were floating laboratories and, as well as being documented and sketched, finds that could be preserved were sent back to France. Lésueur himself developed a close working relationship with the naturalist on board, François Péron, who

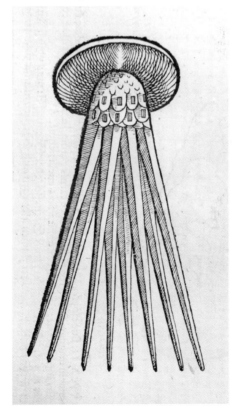

An early illustration of a jellyfish from Conrad Gessner's treatise *Icones animalium* (1560), rotated view. Gessner was a Swiss naturalist, born and educated in Zurich, who attempted to list all the world's animals.

wrote about his finds, while Lésueur drew what they caught. Lésueur's drawings became more professional, in the sense that he learned how best to depict his subjects for scientific analysis, as the relationship developed. The two were pioneers in documenting diversity among jellyfish and as well as studying their morphology they noted their bioluminescence and made observations on their swimming behaviour. On returning to France, the two were commissioned by Napoleon to produce an illustrated account of the voyage. Of Lésueur, Péron said, 'Whatever I applied myself to, describing with care, Lésueur drew or painted with that accuracy and skill that earned him so much honourable approbation.'[4] Most of the drawings and manuscript notes made by them were never published, yet their work was used by others without proper acknowledgement until it was compiled and deposited in the Muséum d'Histoire naturelle in Le Havre by Jacqueline Goy in 1992.[5]

While the zoologist Louis Agassiz was himself an accomplished draftsman, he too relied on illustrators. One, Alfred G. Mayor (formerly Mayer), who was a student of his, showed particular skill in depicting different jellyfish in colour. He co-authored a book with Agassiz on the medusae of the Western Atlantic and together they went on several collecting expeditions to the Caribbean and Oceania. Mayor went on to produce an illustrated three-volume work, *Medusae of the World*, in 1910. There was one particular illustrator that Agassiz came to rely on heavily and that was Antoine Sonrel. I have already stressed how Agassiz attached great importance to observation and it is easy to see how Sonrel's meticulous drawings earned him the respect of the author of *Contributions to the Natural History of the United States of America.* Sonrel's skills are only too evident in his depiction of the lion's mane jellyfish, *Cyanea arctica.* His illustration offers the viewer an intimate and detailed examination of this ethereal creature. The tentacles, though truncated, give the impression of threads in motion, criss-crossing one another but never appearing to be in danger of becoming entangled. The bell of the jellyfish, like a showerhead issuing fine streams of water, sits at the top of the page, while the fine tentacles extend downwards beyond a fold in the paper.

Sonrel's drawings stand in contrast to those of Agassiz's contemporary, Ernst Haeckel, another well-respected figure both in zoological circles and in the world of illustration. The sinuous tentacles are there, but less delicately drawn and instead arranged stylistically on the page along with illustrations of other jellyfish. More attention is given to composition than in Sonrel's drawings and, as Agassiz's biographer Christoph Irmscher suggests, Haeckel appeared intent on forming 'tableaus of flowing lines and perfect symmetry that have more in common with the conventions of *art nouveau* than the organisms he'd observed'.[6] Sonrel was a meticulous, scientific observer while Haeckel was a painter and pattern-maker who wished to emphasize the beauty of his subject, sometimes at the expense of accuracy and colour. Haeckel stood accused of confusing art and science, of letting his imagination run riot, yet in truth he acted as a bridge between the two disciplines and an authority like Darwin recognized his talents and dedication. Haeckel was responsible for depictions of over six hundred species of jellyfish in his *System der Medusen*. There is a touching passage in the book that speaks of his attachment to a particular jellyfish:

Mitrocoma annae belongs to the most delicate of all medusae . . . I enjoyed several happy hours watching the play of her tentacles which hang like blonde hair-ornaments from the rim of the delicate umbrella-cap and which, with the softest movement, would roll up into

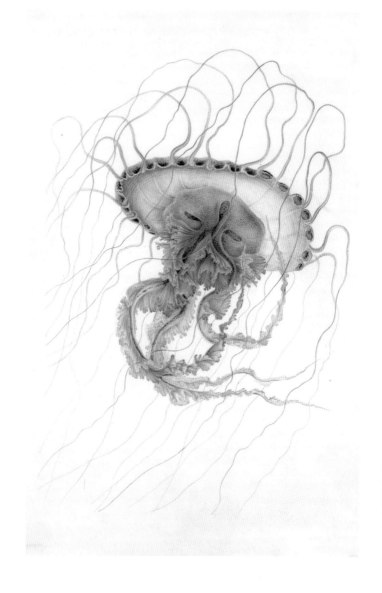

thick, short spirals . . . I name this species the 'Princess of the Eucopiden' as a memorial to my unforgettable, true wife, Anna Sethe . . . who was torn from me through sudden death in 1864.[7]

According to Haeckel's biographer Robert J. Richards, he had a further encounter with another even lovelier jellyfish which he named *Desmonema annasethe*.[8] There is no doubt Haeckel's

Lésueur's depiction of the Atlantic sea nettle, *Chrysaora hysoscella*. Chrysaor was the son of Poseidon and Medusa.

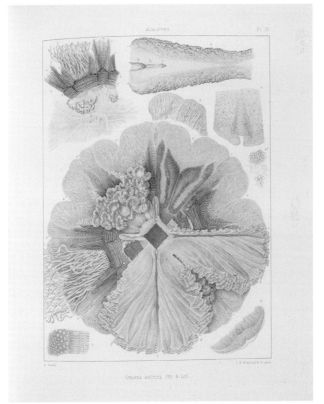

These beautifully executed drawings of *Cyanea arctica* by Antoine Sonrel appear in Agassiz's *Contributions to the Natural History of the United States of America* (1860).

illustrations were a source of inspiration to the art nouveau movement in the late nineteenth and early twentieth centuries. His *Kunstformen der Natur* proved to be a major influence. Émile Gallé, one of the movement's founders, owned a copy and decorated his glass vases with jellyfish that could have come directly from Haeckel's pictures.

Making a record of new species of jellyfish relied on making a pictorial record then and there or preserving the specimen in alcohol or formalin. Unlike vertebrates, jellyfish could not be stuffed and mounted, and unlike insects they could not be pinned to a board. Preserving them in alcohol meant losing some colour and translucency. Apart from making drawings and colour illustrations, the only way to provide a replica of the living animal was to create a model using wax, papier-mâché or, better still, glass. Two Czech lamp-workers, Leopold and Rudolf Blaschka, father and son, were able to do just that.[9] They came from a long line of glass craftsmen. Leopold, the father, developed a technique called 'glass-spinning' which enabled him to create objects of great delicacy and to record in detail what he saw. It is said that during a voyage to America, Leopold's ship was becalmed and he passed the time collecting and drawing marine invertebrates. The evening light shows of bioluminescent sea organisms entranced him, as did the glass-like translucency and the sheer beauty of the jellyfish he saw. He decided to translate into glass several of his own drawings of jellyfish. His skill in working with glass and the same attention to detail was passed on to his son Rudolf. Together father and son worked from illustrations of jellyfish, preserved material and live specimens to create lifelike models that proved invaluable as teaching aids. Haeckel himself lent the Blaschkas some of his own illustrations. The 3D representations in glass proved to be exceedingly popular in educational establishments both in Europe and America. The production of these models coincided with a great expansion in public interest in the natural sciences in the nineteenth century and the opening of several museums where their work was displayed. The Blaschkas' output was prodigious. Louis Agassiz himself formed a collection for teaching purposes which was housed in his Museum of Comparative Anatomy at Harvard, while one of his assistants, Henry Ward, became an agent of the Blaschkas, supplying schools and universities with glass replicas of jellyfish. We know that the Blaschkas both admired and closely followed Haeckel's work and we can see evidence of this in their work. They shared a particular fascination for siphonophores. Models in glass showed different developmental stages of this type of jellyfish as well as the division of labour within each colony. Their blend of artistry and science continues to draw people to the many museums and private collections of their work throughout the world. An archive showing the original illustrations

Leopold and Rudolf Blaschka's glass model of the siphonophore *Physophora magnifica*, 1885.

The Blaschkas' glass model of the hydrozoan *Cladonema radiatum*, 1885.

from which the glass replicas were made can be viewed in the Rakow Research Library at the Corning Museum of Glass in New York State.

The fact that many jellyfish were damaged on being brought to the surface in nets continued to be a problem and acted as a brake to fully understanding these delicate and friable creatures. Observers also experienced difficulty in viewing them in their natural habitat, and those jellyfish inhabiting the deepest recesses of the ocean remained out of reach and invisible. Ever since Jules Verne wrote *Twenty Thousand Leagues Under the Sea* in 1870,

Leopold and
Rudolf Blaschka's
glass model
of *Porpita
mediterranea*, 1885.

interest had been aroused in what lay in the depths. Among the many inspirations that provided Verne with material for his book were the Paris Aquariums constructed for the Paris Exhibition of 1867. Competition existed between European cities to build aquariums housing varied and often exotic marine creatures. It is doubtful whether many of them contained jellyfish, since these were proving too delicate for such containers, but the French photographer Étienne-Jules Marey was able to capture the movement of jellyfish in his Naples aquarium by the sea. As William Firebrace in his book *Memo for Nemo* says, 'The writhing medusa, several million years old, no doubt unconscious of its star potential, was leading the way out of the aquarium and towards the silver screen.'[10]

Witnessing jellyfish in their natural environment was delayed until the 1930s when the first manned descent into 'the deep' was attempted. William Beebe achieved this off the coast of Bermuda encased in a steel sphere suspended by a cable that, in turn, was tethered to a floating barge.[11] There were just three viewing ports in the capsule, and small ones at that, and just enough space for two submariners. The oxygen that was pumped in was sufficient to keep two people alive for eight hours and the carbon dioxide they exhaled was extracted using calcium chloride and soda lime. What Beebe saw in his 'bathysphere' was communicated by telephone to his assistant, Gloria Hollister, who was responsible for transcribing his words. The fact that there was no photographic record of what he saw meant his findings, documented in his book *Half Mile Down*, were viewed with some suspicion. Nevertheless, some of the commonest organisms he reported seeing were medusae and comb jellies. The latter could readily be distinguished by their ciliate motion compared to the pulsatile movements of the medusae. Siphonophores were even recorded at depths of 600 m (2,000 ft). Several were observed to emit a

A spaceship from earth encounters deadly jellyfish-like creatures in the novelette *Dragons of Space* (1930) by Aladra Septama.

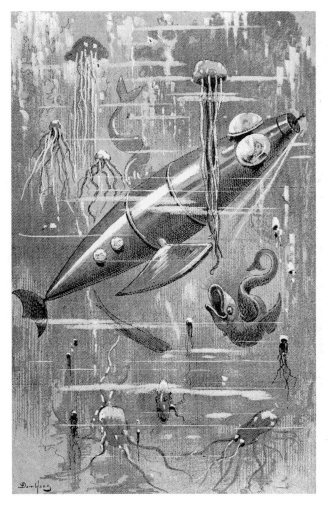

A futuristic
submarine
from an edition
of *La Science
illustrée* (1875).

pale yellow light. At this depth Beebe described 'a feeling of utter loneliness and isolation akin to that which might grip the first to venture upon the moon or Venus'. His was the first glimpse of a world that had never before been entered by humankind.

Beebe's premature retirement in 1934 left a hiatus in the manned exploration of the ocean's depths until 1943 when the Frenchman Jacques Cousteau, along with Émile Gagnan, invented the aqualung. This device enabled divers to spend longer periods in the water and was followed by the 'diving-saucer', a prototype of the modern submarine. In 1951 Cousteau began a series of trips on board his boat *Calypso* in which his new technology could be tested, along with the use of an underwater camera. Cousteau was by now collaborating with Harold Edgerton, also known as 'Papa Flash', who was to prove to be a pioneer in deep-sea camera work. In 1956 a highly acclaimed film, *The Silent World*, came out about the inhabitants of the ocean. Cousteau was using his diving-saucer to explore the continental shelf, but its operating depth was only 300 m (1,000 ft). From these depths, images of marine creatures were broadcast onto television screens and could be viewed from the comfort of an armchair. The 'illustrator's nightmare' had been at least partially solved. There was now a way of focusing the public's attention on creatures that had hitherto never been seen or had evaded capture. With the advent of video technology, colour and movement could also be recorded. It wasn't plain sailing, however. A degree of colour and contrast was lost the deeper you went into the water, though by using flash some colour could be restored.

Cousteau was also anxious to promote underwater living, bringing 'style and colour to the bottom of the oceans'. Another Frenchman, the architect Jacques Rougerie, designed a subsea village, a place for training astronauts who needed to acclimatize to a life under cramped conditions. His design, particularly the

Observing jellyfish from the Nautilus. A scene from Jules Verne, *Twenty Thousand Leagues Under the Sea* (1870).

domed tents tethered by cables to the seabed surrounding a central structure potentially housing 250 individuals, bore a close resemblance to jellyfish.[12] It was never built. Nor was another project, again inspired by jellyfish, consisting of a luminous hemisphere able to cruise at considerable depths, from which a spherical laboratory could be dispatched. His constructions belonged more to the world of fantasy than reality.

Of the deeper layers of the sea, a world where light did not penetrate, knowledge was scant. To begin with, what sort of animal life, if any, existed there? Could jellyfish themselves survive many thousands of feet below the ocean's surface where the pressure was that much greater than in the sunlit surface waters? Could they be viewed from a sufficiently robust submersible?

Beebe had previously remarked how 'schools of jellyfish throbbed their energetic way through life' and past his own bathysphere's viewing ports. Would they still be visible lower down? As a result of constructing a new submersible, *Alvin*, capable of carrying passengers, it became possible to reach depths of around 1,800 m (6,000 ft). Armed with cameras, Robert Ballard and Fred Grassle, two deep-sea explorers, led an expedition to explore the Galápagos Rift. What they saw was shown on a television programme, *Dive to the Edge of Creation.* Among the strange and exotic creatures such as crabs and tube worms were 'a clutch of mysterious dandelions'. These appeared at the edge of hydrothermal vents at a depth of around 2,400 m (8,000 ft) and were attached 'like tethered hot-air balloons' by means of numerous tentacles to rocks. They were jellyfish, and Philip Pugh, the leading authority on siphonophores, was able to place them in this grouping and to document their many unusual features such as large, gas-secreting pneumatophores and cormidia arranged in spirals around a central corm.[13]

To this day, scientists continue to be surprised by the oddity and profusion of jellyfish to be seen in the deepest layers of the ocean. Television programmes such as *Blue Planet II* have been instrumental in educating the public about life in 'the deep' and how we need to be concerned about preserving life here as well as in the upper zones of the sea. Among the endangered species are, of course, jellyfish.

Sampling fragile creatures from the sea has undergone great improvement in recent years. Instead of trawling with nets, which can be destructive to delicate sea creatures, they can now be sampled under direct vision. One technique for doing this, known as 'blue-water diving', involves using a buoy and weighted tethers to enable divers to descend to 50 m (165 ft) with a degree of safety. There, material can be collected by hand. Steven Haddock eloquently describes the experience:

> there is no bottom, there is blue in every direction. No fixed points to orientate or to hold your eye. If it is a clear day and there is good visibility, the sea above looks like silvery ripples and the light blue water to your side fades to the navy blue of the depths. At night nothing can be seen but the beams of dive lights and the animals that come into their luminous cones. When the lights are off, each diver is surrounded by a cloud of bioluminescent particles and even the wave of a hand makes the water startlingly bright.[14]

As well as 'blue-water diving', there are submersibles that can be modified to collect animals at depth, either manned submarines or remotely operated vehicles (ROVs). These have been put to use by explorers such as Alexander Semenov to show both the beauty and the alien-like qualities of the jellyfish that live there. His *Aquatilis* expedition includes a team of scientists, divers and photographers from Moscow State University White Sea Biological Station. Their stated aim is to explore the world's oceans in search of new species. The images that have come from Semenov's team are stunning, displaying the complexity of the zooplankton, particularly among the jellyfish living in the abyssal depths of the ocean.[15] Other scientists too are contributing to our understanding of this least-explored part of the planet. Over the course of several expeditions to the Arctic from 2010 onwards, the National Oceanic and Atmospheric Administration, for example, came across a surprisingly diverse collection of different jellyfish in polar waters.[16] One example was the colourful pantachogon jellyfish, which incorporates oil globules into its body. Elsewhere, deep in the Mariana Trench in the Pacific Ocean, a team from NOAA captured on film another bizarre jellyfish. Red and yellow lights from inside the globular bell give it the appearance of a spacecraft. Identified as a hydromedusa of the genus *Crossota*, this jellyfish was discovered at a depth of 3,700 m (12,000 ft). Small wonder that craft capable of exploring the abyssal depths are becoming the next 'must have' toy among the seriously wealthy! Ninety-five per cent of the oceans remains unseen by human eyes and is likely to yield many more animal secrets for those prepared to go in search of them.

Today, images of jellyfish can be found everywhere on paper, canvas, glass and celluloid, as well as digitally on our television

A deep-water jellyfish of the genus *Crossota*, a hydromedusa without a polyp phase in its life cycle.

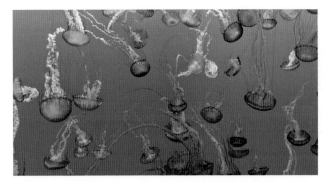

screens. An image of a lion's mane jellyfish taken by George Stoyle, with fish sheltering in its tentacles, took first prize in the 2016 British Wildlife Photography awards. Such photographs bring into focus the detail and colour of these creatures, but a further modern advance – the Kreisel tank – has proved useful in bringing these animals to the attention of a wider public. The tank lacks corners and is often large, round or oval in cross-section with a laminar flow water system that sustains the jellyfish within and keeps them active. The water in the tank can be filtered, heated or cooled. The particular design involving no hard edges was badly needed so that delicate creatures like jellyfish were less likely to injure themselves in captivity. More and more aquaria are now displaying jellyfish and a list of these can be found in Appendix 2. Now the illustrator's medium has switched from ink and paper to the camera lens. The images seen in books such as Christian Sardet's *Plankton: Wonders of the Drifting World* and Per Robert Flood's *Fjord* give us much more accurate, close-up pictures of jellyfish than ever before. That is not to say that Haeckel's paintings or the beautiful coloured drawings which complement, say, Sir Frederick Russell's *The Medusae of the British Isles* no longer merit our attention. There is still a place for both types of illustration.

5 Jellyfish Culture

Earlier I examined the way the Medusa myth coloured our view of the animal so that it was seen both as an object of fascination and as a creature to be feared. Here, I want to explore the contribution the animal itself has made to our culture in terms of art and design, literature, modern media and cuisine.

When we think of the jellyfish we often confuse it with that other tentacled creature, the octopus. The two animals couldn't be more different anatomically and in terms of their behaviour, yet the predatory tentacles of both often interlock in our minds. One obvious distinguishing feature is the presence or absence of eyes. A stare from an octopus implies a level of awareness and seemingly a willingness to communicate. Absence of eyes implies the opposite, creating a barrier between us and the jellyfish. Adding eyes to the body of the jellyfish (and here I choose to ignore the small, light-sensitive receptors that can be found in jellyfish) immediately animates it, sometimes in a disconcerting way. This is illustrated in a picture by Elissaveta Dandali called *No Tears for the Creatures of the Night*. The eyes belong to the octopus, the tentacles to the jellyfish.

While we commonly attribute human traits, emotions and intentions to animals, this appears not to be the case with jellyfish and goes some way to explaining why jellyfish are largely absent from early depictions of marine life. Examining Minoan

Elissaveta Dandali, *No Tears for the Creatures of the Night*, 2015.

pottery of the 'marine style' shows vases covered in miscellaneous sea creatures, but no definite jellyfish. The most illustrated creature is the octopus, closely followed by the dolphin and varieties of fish. The same is true of Roman art. Other sea creatures populate the tessellated pavements and the only connection to jellyfish is through Medusa, the Gorgon sister whose gaze turns humans to stone.

Apart from a few engravings of the Portuguese man-of-war, there is precious little jellyfish imagery until we reach the Enlightenment, when travel to foreign parts and long ocean voyages aroused interest in animal diversity. Even then, the fact that jellyfish were difficult to capture in one piece and preserve created problems for the artist. Haeckel's illustrations made a significant impact, but it was the advent of underwater photography that resulted in a substantial number of images of jellyfish being made available to the public, and it was only then that the subtleties of their movement began to be appreciated. Artists, seeing them

Detail from
a mosaic floor
showing Medusa's
head. Rome,
c. 115–50.

94

close up, began to draw inspiration from these creatures and it was to demonstrate the link between art and nature that Monterey Aquarium in 2002 mounted a special exhibition of jellyfish which attracted over ten million visitors and won several awards.[1] 'Jellies: Living Art' featured 25 species of jellyfish and proved to be the longest-running exhibit since the aquarium opened in 1964. Apart from live jellyfish, there were works of art, videos, interactive displays and installations. The exhibition amounted to a celebration of the beauty of jellyfish and was organized around three main areas: shape and size, rhythm and movement, and colour and pattern. An installation in glass by Dale Chihuly demonstrated the colours and translucent properties of jellyfish, while Cork Marcheschi, an artist famous for his light sculptures, focused

Ceiling decoration in the Villa Medusa in Jena, Germany, based on a drawing of a jellyfish by Haeckel.

attention on the way jellyfish moved using large lava lamps filled with inert gases. Some of the Blaschkas' own glass models, together with a display of scientific illustrations, emphasized the sheer diversity of jellyfish. Music appropriate to each area was also provided and walls featured quotations from Pablo Neruda, Jimi Hendrix and Rachel Carson alongside paintings from artists as diverse as Michelangelo and David Hockney.

The dome-like bell of the jellyfish medusa with its limpid, dependent tentacles has made an impact on sculptors as well as artists. Prince Albert I of Monaco was so taken by jellyfish that he had a glass chandelier made in the likeness of one for his 'Temple of the Sea' in Monaco, now the Oceanographic Museum. It was designed by Constant Roux and modelled on an illustration in Haeckel's *Kunstformen der Natur*, a jellyfish called *Rhopilema frida*. Timothy Horn, an Australian artist, also took the engravings of Ernst Haeckel as his starting point and has created chandeliers made of transparent silicone rubber. His huge *Discomedusae* (2004), measuring 2.7 m (9 ft) across, is lit internally and, while constructed in Boston, now hangs in the foyer of the Hawke Building in the University of South Australia, Adelaide, like some alien creature from space. Smaller luminous jellyfish have since appeared in shop windows along Rodeo Drive in Beverly Hills, and lampshades and hangings resembling jellyfish have become popular items for the discerning shopper worldwide. For Ranim Orouk it was a bloom of jellyfish that proved inspirational for a piece named *Glow*, selected for the Middle East Emergent Designer Prize in 2016. Light played on spheres of glass in the shape of jellyfish bells, while curved acrylic rods served to remind us of their tentacles. The varied colours of jellyfish have proved

Discomedusae by Timothy Horn, 2004, on display at the Hawke building, University of South Australia, Adelaide.

to be important in the work of sculptor Daniela Forti, where coloured glass is used to form tentacles which hang like drips of melting ice cream from a central disc. The British glass artist Helen Dyne, working in translucent coloured glass, captures the beauty of jellyfish as light penetrates her sculptures, while Marzio Rusconi Clerici from Milan simulates their fluid motion by using thermoformed plastic. Other materials, from plants to stiffened lace to coloured knitting wool, have been used to create jellyfish art. Dorit Schubert from Dresden works with nylon and silver to produce delicate earrings in the shape of medusae.

Among the most popular representations of jellyfish today are glass-in-glass sculptures. In the late 1980s an artist called Richard Satava, watching jellyfish in an aquarium, was inspired to make likenesses of them inside glass shapes and they were sold in galleries and gift shops throughout America. In the 1990s another artist from Hawaii, Christopher Lowry, began making similar sculptures. Satava filed a lawsuit against Lowry, accusing him of copyright infringement. Satava was successful, but the decision was appealed and the decision of the district court was subsequently reversed. Satava's sculptures were deemed to

Helen Dyne's jellyfish sculpture in glass.

Daniela Forti's coloured glass sculpture inspired by jellyfish.

combine several unprotectable ideas and standard elements. They were seen as being the common property of all and Satava was denied copyright for his own use.[2]

As far as architecture is concerned, an example of innovative design inspired by nature can be seen in a model made by Michael Sorkin for a hotel in Tianjin, China. It is unequivocally a jellyfish medusa. The prize for biomimicry however must surely go to Alanna Howe and Alexander Hespe, whose contribution to the

Jellyfish table lamp designed by Marzio Rusconi Clerici for Fragile Edizioni, 2016.

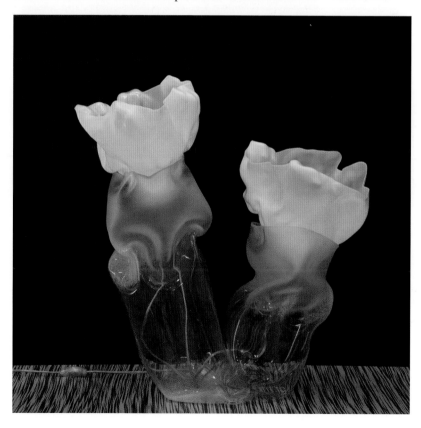

2010 Venice Biennale, 'Siph City', used a siphonophore as its starting point.[3] In a competition to design something for the future, the two took as their subject 'The Underwater City'. Drawing upon the arrangement of zooids in a Portuguese man-of-war, they designed a floating city. Below the water surface were pods serving different functions. Residences, farms and recreational facilities were separated out while remaining in contact with one

A glass-in-glass paperweight designed by Hübsch.

Jellyfish hotel, designed by Michael Sorkin Studio, New York, 2010.

another. Trailing appendages, akin to tentacles, collected energy from the waves and transformed salt water into fresh water by a process of desalination. In stormy conditions, the pods stayed below the water surface, but in sunny, calmer conditions they floated to the surface using the sun's rays as a source of power. The idea may seem fanciful, but with human population growth leading to overcrowding on dry land, ocean cities may become a reality in the not too distant future and, by examining designs provided by nature, Howe and Hespe point one way towards solving some of the problems facing us on the planet.

Programmes like *Blue Planet II* have promoted a culture of concern about our oceans and their inhabitants. Gelatinous creatures, notably those living in the dark, abyssal depths of the sea, feature prominently, but outside documentaries about the oceans jellyfish make few appearances on our screens or in the cinema. A notable exception comes from the work of James Cameron, filmmaker and explorer. Some of the computer-generated animals in *Avatar* bear a striking resemblance to jellyfish. Cameron based his vision of Pandora's forests on what he saw in his sea expeditions. His 'woodsprite', for example, is similar to a small, deep-sea jellyfish, yet floats on the wind like the seed heads of a dandelion.[4] Cameron, who directed *Titanic* and *The Abyss*, has clearly been influenced by the sea and the creatures it contains. He himself piloted a deep-sea submersible, the *Deepsea Challenger*, equipped with 3D cameras, to the deepest point in the ocean when he explored the Mariana Trench in 2012. More than 9 km (6 mi.) below the surface of the water he witnessed a host of gelatinous animals including jellyfish; we might anticipate more medusa-like creatures in future films by him.

Jellyfish make an appearance in TV and films for children. *The Octonauts*, a popular British children's television series, includes a jellyfish which manages to get its long tentacles tangled in the *Octopod*'s engine, while in another episode two of the main characters become encircled by a glowing siphonophore.[5] Jellyfish likewise appear as minor characters in *Finding Nemo*, a popular computer-animated film featuring a clownfish called Marlin and a blue tang called Dory.[6] Marlin and Dory find themselves in a forest of jellyfish and escape by bouncing off the jellyfish, but are stung in the process.

The movie *Jellyfish*, which won the Caméra d'Or at Cannes, while not featuring a single jellyfish, follows the lives of three women in Tel Aviv.[7] Like jellyfish, the three appear not to know where they are heading, drifting through life and finding themselves driven in different directions. The film begins and ends with a solitary, rather enigmatic red-haired girl. She appears alone and lost on a beach wearing a flotation ring. The final scene shows

Marlin and Dory encounter jellyfish in *Finding Nemo* (2003).

her returning to the sea despite attempts to rescue her. Whether she is the metaphorical jellyfish is open to speculation.

Understandably, the varied colours and ethereal quality of jellyfish have influenced the world of fashion. Giant feathered hats resembling jellyfish, the brainchild of designer Pierpaolo Piccioli, dominated the Valentino Spring 2018 Couture show, while a blue coat dress sporting coloured medusae from the Gucci fashion house appeared on the catwalk in 2016. Textiles featuring jellyfish, such as those made by Reiko Sudo, have proved popular, while Alexander McQueen, who was quoted in the V&A retrospective 'Savage Beauty' (2011) as saying 'There is no better designer than nature,' drew much of his inspiration from the sea and included jellyfish designs in his collections.

As far as literature is concerned, there are surprisingly few allusions to jellyfish in fiction. Probably the best-known example is Arthur Conan Doyle's short story 'The Adventure of the Lion's Mane'.[8] In it, Sherlock Holmes, by now retired to the coast, investigates the death of a local schoolteacher whose body has been discovered close to the shoreline with livid weals on the skin. The victim, we are told, died in great pain muttering the words 'the lion's mane'. Suspicion falls on a fellow teacher and Holmes, on this occasion not assisted by Dr Watson, is wrong-footed, believing the victim hadn't been in the water since the towel he was carrying was dry. Following a copycat attack on someone else, this time not fatal, Holmes becomes suspicious that the injuries in both cases were inflicted by *Cyanea capillata*, the lion's mane jellyfish, which he spies in the water nearby. His intuition proves correct. The lion's mane jellyfish is one of the commonest large jellyfish in our coastal waters and boasts a mass of long, hair-like

Jellyfish hat designed by Pierpaolo Piccioli, Valentino's creative director, in 2018.

tentacles. Its sting is painful, but rarely fatal. In this case the fatality arose because the victim had a pre-existing heart condition. Conan Doyle considered it one of his best short stories and it has certainly enjoyed enduring popularity among his readers.

When Jules Verne wrote *Twenty Thousand Leagues Under the Sea* in 1870, knowledge of the undersea world was sketchy. Through the window of his imaginary submarine the *Nautilus*, Verne offered the reader a glimpse of an unfamiliar world populated by marauding octopuses and strange sea creatures. In one illustration from the book, jellyfish float like parasols above the heads of the crew as they take a stroll along the ocean floor. The text is full of detailed descriptions of zoophytes, along with their Latin names, including the compass jellyfish, *Chrysaora hysoscella*:

> Some of these jellyfish were shaped like very smooth, semispheric parasols with russet stripes and fringes of twelve neat festoons. Others looked like upside-down baskets from which wide leaves and long red twigs were gracefully trailing. They swam with quiverings of their four leaf-like arms, letting the opulent tresses of their tentacles dangle in the drifts. I wanted to preserve a few specimens of these delicate zoophytes, but they were merely clouds, shadows, illusions, melting and evaporating outside their native element.[9]

The captain of the *Nautilus*, Nemo, at odds with the terrestrial world of man, had adopted the sea as his refuge. He appears like some alien jellyfish himself, 'reflected like a mirror image in the encapsulated specimens he so carefully gathers and exhibits behind glass'. The book has been made into a film on several occasions and the one directed by Stuart Paton in 1916 was the first motion picture to be filmed underwater.

Aimed at 'curious kids anywhere' is Ali Benjamin's book *The Thing About Jellyfish*. Woven into the narrative are facts about jellyfish and pictures of the Pacific sea nettle, *Chrysaora fuscescens*, though the main player is, in fact, a box jellyfish. The story is a study of childhood grief. The young narrator's best friend, an accomplished swimmer, dies in a drowning incident and there is a reluctance on the part of the central character to accept her death as being an accident. Instead, her friend is convinced she died from a jellyfish sting and sets out to prove her suspicion. In the process, she learns a lot about jellyfish and even more about herself. The novel was nominated for a National Book Award. The author admits to being captivated by jellyfish and she makes an

Walking along the seabed. A scene from Jules Verne's *Twenty Thousand Leagues Under the Sea* (1870).

interesting comparison in the novel between the motion of jelly-fish and the beating of a human heart: 'it's their pulse, the way they contract swiftly, then release. Like a ghost heart – a heart you can see through, right into some other world where every-thing you ever lost has gone to hide.'[10]

References to jellyfish occasionally pop up in modern novels. For example, in *Gone Girl*, Gillian Flynn compares soulmates to 'conjoined jellyfish' and goes on to describe why: 'They have no hard edges with each other, no spiny conflicts . . . filling each other's spaces with liquidity.'[11] In *Alias Grace*, Margaret Atwood compares a group of nineteenth-century ladies, visitors to a peni-tentiary, wearing stiff wire crinolines beneath their dresses, to the bells of jellyfish drifting through the sea.[12]

Jellyfish tend to feature more in poems than in prose. In 'The Borough', published in 1810, George Crabbe, who was both a poet and a naturalist, celebrated 'those living jellies which the flesh inflame, fierce as a nettle, and from that its name'.[13] In a footnote to the poem, he refers specifically to a particular small jellyfish, oval in shape, with serrated, longitudinal markings. It is almost certainly a comb jelly. Seeing these as the product of a divine hand, he wrote:

There's not a gem
Wrought by man's art to be compared to them:
Soft, brilliant, tender, through the wave they glow
And make the moonbeams brighter where they flow.[14]

Guillaume Apollinaire in his poem 'La Méduse' appears less enamoured of jellyfish:

Méduses, malheureuses têtes
Aux chevelures violettes

Medusas, miserable heads
Whose hair is violet

but finds he has something in common with them, namely a love
of stormy weather:

Vous vous plaisez dans les tempêtes
    Et je m'y plais comme vous faites.

You are happy in stormy weather
    And I am happy then like you[15]

The American Mark Doty, in his poem 'Difference', is attracted
by their shifting shapes in the water:

every one does something unlike:
this one a balloon
open at both ends . . .
This one a rolled condom
Or a plastic purse swallowing itself,
that one a Tiffany shade.[16]

The children's poet Michael Rosen finds similarity between a
jellyfish and a child at a party, dancing and 'waving its frilly
underwear'.[17] Karl Pilkington, the poet, bemoans the fact jellyfish
can't be eaten 'with chips and mushy peas',[18] though they are
eaten in considerable amounts all over Southeast Asia – in China
they are even considered a delicacy. The edible ones lend themselves to a calorie-controlled diet. Not only do they have low
calorific values and negligible fat content, but protein and min-
erals are the richest components. Their consumption is thought
by some to be beneficial to such widely divergent conditions as

hypertension, arthritis and digestive disorders. However, there is as yet no scientific proof of their effectiveness.

Natalie Harris-Spencer in her lifestyle blog *The Edible Editor* offers a description of what it is like to eat jellyfish: 'Soft to the tongue; slow, steady hints of miso soup and spring onions, a simple smokey flavour, like fish stock. Once bitten, traces of toughness and an imagined squeak reverberating from tooth to ear. A sudden sharp suggestion of chilli.'[19]

In truth, jellyfish lack much taste and are eaten more for their texture than their flavour, though they can act as a vehicle for different flavours. They need to be processed soon after they are caught since they disintegrate rapidly out of water. The umbrella and oral arms of the jellyfish are separated immediately and cleaned with seawater. Mucus and reproductive parts are then removed. What remains is repeatedly soaked in a mix of brine and alum and then dried with a coating of salt. The salted jellyfish can then be left to dry at room temperature for two days. The cured jellyfish can be stored for up to a year, 'revived' by adding

Jellyfish harvesting. The jellyfish are caught in the north Andaman Sea, salted and exported to China and Japan.

A traditional Chinese favourite: jellyfish served with sesame oil and chilli sauce.

water, then cut into strips and scalded. Cured jellyfish tends to have a crispy, crunchy texture. Cooked with vegetables or meat, or served cold with a dressing of vinegar, oil or soy sauce, it forms an ingredient in many East Asian recipes. A wedding in China often includes a jellyfish salad while in Japan shredded jellyfish is traditionally served with vinegar as an appetizer.

The list of edible jellyfish is a long one but they mainly belong to the genus *Rhizostoma*. Commonly eaten varieties include the cannonball jellyfish, the blue blubber jellyfish and the flame jellyfish. Mostly they are found in estuaries. China was the first country to process jellyfish for human consumption, but with the abundance of cannonball jellyfish in the coastal waters of the States, we could see more of this species on our plates in the future.

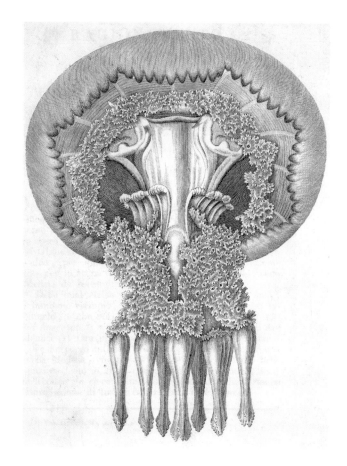

An edible jellyfish of the genus *Rhizostoma*, here from an 1843 engraving by Raffaele Estevan.

Nomura's jellyfish, *Nemopilema nomurai*, has even been made into ice cream, while in Britain the ice-cream maker Charlie Harry Francis has created a glow-in-the-dark ice cream using synthesized jellyfish protein. It is however expensive to produce. To accommodate Western tastes, food writer and presenter Stefan Gates has a recipe for jellyfish burgers that are served with a sweet chilli sauce, while jellyfish crisps have been made by soaking jellyfish in alcohol and allowing the liquid to evaporate. According to Mie Thorborg Pedersen, writing in the *International Journal of Gastronomy and Food Science*, these paper-thin, crunchy discs resemble ordinary potato crisps but contain much less fat.[20] They do however need flavouring and the salt content can be high.

The world's leading consumer of jellyfish is currently Japan, which imports huge quantities each year from the Philippines, Malaysia and other Southeast Asian countries. The jellyfish industry is governed by considerable fluctuations in the size of the catch, the reasons for which are poorly understood, but the market has the potential for expansion should culinary habits change in the West. Silvio Greco of the University of Gastronomic Sciences promoted jellyfish at the 2017 Slow Fish Festival in Genoa, arguing that their increasing numbers (he instances at least four times as many in the Mediterranean now as in 2004) could be exploited if only we could perceive jellyfish as potentially healthy food. 'Man', he says, 'must be the new predator of jellyfish' now that their natural predators, tuna and turtles, are diminishing.[21]

From the examples quoted, the influence of jellyfish on our own culture could be said to have been widespread yet modest. I suggest this is because they are largely invisible, but also because they fail to endear themselves to us. As we scour the planet for new visual and culinary experiences, assisted by a better understanding of the world they live in, it seems likely their influence will increase. Their beauty is undeniable and there is another property too that is overlooked. That is their transience. Like flowers, they bloom and fade and appear to leave nothing behind. Being ephemeral creatures, they provide a reminder of our own impermanence on Planet Earth.

6 Light, Death and Immortality

Human beings dream of life everlasting . . . but
most of them want it on earth and not in heaven.
Tennessee Williams, *Cat on a Hot Tin Roof*

The woods decay, the woods decay and fall,
The vapours weep their burthen to the ground,
Man comes and tills the field and lies beneath,
And after many a summer dies the swan.
Me only cruel immortality
Consumes: I wither slowly in thine arms.
Alfred, Lord Tennyson, 'Tithonus'

It is commonly said of animals that sting, creatures like wasps
and jellyfish, that they have no purpose other than to annoy us
and that humanity would be better off without them. Apart from
their importance as part of the food web, on which we all depend,
one can discover something of benefit to humanity in almost
every type of animal, and this is certainly the case with jellyfish.
Take three examples: two where jellyfish research resulted in a
Nobel Prize for the discoverer and one where a particular type of
jellyfish may hold the key to immortality.

Pliny the Elder in his *Natural History* mentions, among other
luminescent creatures, a jellyfish he calls *Pulmo marinus*. He
describes how a walking stick when rubbed against its body is
capable of emitting light like a torch.[1] The particular species is
likely to have been *Pelagia noctiluca*, widespread in the Mediterranean. In its undisturbed state it doesn't glow, but when rubbed,
even out of water, it can luminesce. Bioluminescence, the production and emission of light from a living organism, is common
in the sea and is thought to have evolved independently on several occasions. It occurs across a range of animals from bacteria

The mauve stinger,
Pelagia noctiluca.
When startled it
leaves a trail of
glowing mucus
behind it.

to fish and this includes certain jellyfish. In the early days, the term 'phosphorescence' was used to describe the same phenomenon, though strictly speaking phosphorescence is seen only when something is itself being illuminated, whereas bioluminescence refers to the production of light through a chemical reaction.

While the chemistry of bioluminescence is unknown in most organisms, this is not true of the crystal jellyfish, *Aequorea victoria*, which has yielded both a luminescent protein, aequorin, and a fluorescent molecule named green fluorescent protein, or GFP. Both are proving useful in biomedical research. So important was the discovery of GFP as a 'tagging tool' in researching the behaviour of cells that it resulted in the awarding of the Nobel Prize in Chemistry in 2008 jointly to Osamu Shimomura, Martin Chalfie and Roger Tsien of the United States for the contribution they made to the understanding of the underlying chemistry.[2] *Aequorea victoria* is a jellyfish found off the west coast of North America, notably in Puget Sound, Washington State. It is virtually colourless and emits light only from around the margin of its bell. Around three hundred light organs, or photophores, give off pinpricks of green light. This light is initially blue and derived from the aequorin molecule. The blue light energy produced by the aequorin is absorbed by the green fluorescent protein, which re-emits the energy as green light. To isolate even the smallest quantities of GFP proved to be painstaking work, but this protein was to become one of the most important tools in bioscience. As a result of its use, ways have been developed to allow scientists to watch cellular processes that were previously invisible.

It is estimated that half of all jellyfish are bioluminescent, particularly those that live at depth in the oceans where light does not penetrate. The function of this isn't always clear but the presumption is that it is a means of communication and can serve both as a defence against predators and as a way of attracting

The crystal jellyfish, *Aequorea victoria*, source of the luminescent protein aequorin and the fluorescent molecule green fluorescent protein (GFP).

prey. Bright flashes of light are able to startle predators, while scattered particles of light mimicking smaller plankton can confuse predators. Mention has already been made in a previous chapter of a certain deep-water siphonophore, *Crossota*, which uses red fluorescent lures to attract its prey. This jellyfish lives in total darkness and generates its light internally from its own photophores. Still others manufacture a luminescent slime capable of attaching itself to a predator, so rendering it vulnerable to other predators. What precise purpose bioluminescence serves in *Aequorea* isn't known but if the medusa is handled and shaken gently (the sting of this jellyfish is imperceptible), a ring of green luminescence lasting just a few seconds occurs at the bell's edge.

The helmet jellyfish, *Periphylla periphylla*, may use bioluminescence to confuse predators.

In 1985 the photo-protein aequorin was successfully cloned. Likewise, the gene for green fluorescent protein was sequenced. Sequencing GFP proved interesting. The protein folded itself into a barrel shape, creating a fluorescing structure that didn't require any additional factor (unlike aequorin).[3] The gene

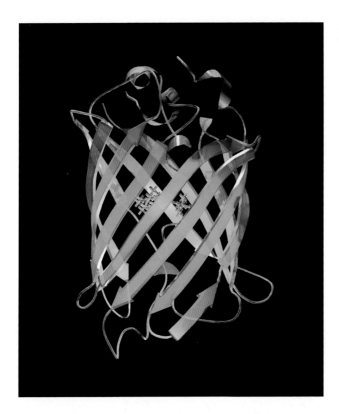

Structure of the GFP molecule.

sequences that code for the GFP protein in the jellyfish can be introduced into viruses, bacteria or even directly into experimental animals. This means that whenever the recipient gene is turned on, so is the introduced GFP gene. Incorporated into a virus, GFP is able to highlight those cells infected by the virus. Incorporated into a bacterium, it can show exactly where the bacterium goes on its travels. Incorporated into an experimental animal, it can show which cells are 'turned on' by a particular gene. By introducing GFP into the cell of an embryo, all the cells

A fluorescent transgenic mouse with the jellyfish gene that codes for GFP. A virus is used to introduce the gene into a fertilized mouse egg. The mouse's skin fluoresces green in blue light.

that are subsequently derived from that cell are effectively labelled. In this way it becomes possible to see which cells survive in a bone marrow graft tagged with GFP, to work out where tumour metastasis arises, and to produce a fluorescent rabbit and mouse – though that was a more frivolous outcome!

The discovery of fluorescent proteins in one jellyfish led to a search for other naturally occurring proteins with similar properties, particularly those that might operate in the longer wavelength range, since these might permit deeper imaging of living tissue. Understanding the chemistry and structure of naturally occurring GFPs and other fluorescent molecules, for example from corals, has enabled scientists to play around with critical protein sequences. Now there exists a large palette of fluorescent proteins in a range of colours and intensities that can be used together in different combinations. Advances in microscopy have also meant it is possible to attach these fluorescent proteins to a variety of sub-cellular structures and watch how they interact with one another within single cells. Green fluorescent protein has certainly opened up a Pandora's box of possibilities that ultimately should prove useful to humanity.

Another jellyfish, this time the colonial siphonophore *Physalia physalis*, was responsible for another Nobel Prize being awarded, this time in Medicine. Charles Richet was persuaded to investigate its sting by no less a person than Prince Albert I of Monaco, a patron of oceanography. His royal yacht, *Princesse Alice II*, with a laboratory on board stocked with experimental animals, set sail for the Cape Verde Islands to harvest this jellyfish. The effects of *Physalia*'s sting were tested on the animals on board and the results proved sufficiently interesting for the work to continue on dry land, this time using venom of similar composition from a sea anemone, which could be more easily accessed. The effects of different doses of the venom on dogs were explored in the expectation that small inoculations of the venom would protect the

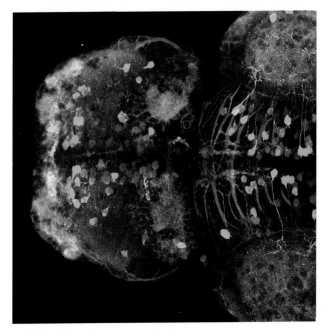

View of a zebrafish brain with some nerve cells, shown in green, highlighted by GFP.

animal from future exposure. The reverse proved to be the case. Those animals that recovered from the initial dose, when challenged again, died and this proved to be the outcome whatever the dose of venom used. The process was termed 'anaphylaxis' by Richet.[4] It proved to be an immune response and demonstrated that immune reactions could have adverse effects, as we now know only too well from the increasing frequency of deaths from ingesting foodstuffs to which certain individuals are strongly allergic. The discovery of anaphylaxis was rewarded with a Nobel

A chalk drawing of the moon jellyfish, *Aurelia aurita*, often used in experiments.

Prize in 1913 and later Monaco commemorated the event with a series of stamps in which the prince, Charles Richet and his colleague Paul Portier figure, together with the yacht *La Physalie*. It is now recognized that anaphylaxis is triggered by an allergen and the only certain way to protect against it is to avoid exposure to that particular allergen.

While we ought to be thankful to jellyfish for our understanding of the processes that exist in our own bodies, their potential contribution to humanity does not end there. The regenerative properties of polyps have been known since Abraham Trembley's early observations of *Hydra* in the first half of the eighteenth century. It was subsequently found that the ability to regenerate an injured part extended to jellyfish polyps and immature jellyfish (ephyrae). More recently, Michael Abrams and others, working with ephyrae of the moon jellyfish, *Aurelia aurita*, discovered a different process of self-repair.[5] In response to injury, the jellyfish ephyrae reorganized themselves so as to regain their radial symmetry. This process, known as 'symmetrization', was usually completed in less than 48 hours. It appeared to be advantageous to the animal since ephyrae that had 'symmetrized' continued to grow into symmetrical jellyfish while ephyrae that did not 'symmetrize' developed abnormally and were unable to swim. One might speculate that fast reorganization in order to regain function might occur in other animals. It is known, for example, that nerve cells in humans can reorganize themselves following a stroke in the body's attempt to repair the damage done. Understanding the mechanism involved better could be of potential benefit to sufferers.

The story of *Turritopsis* goes back to 1988 when a young German scientist called Christian Sommer was collecting small marine organisms off the coast of Portofino on the Italian Riviera.[6] He noticed how one jellyfish in particular appeared to 'age in reverse'.

Instead of proceeding in an orderly way through the normal stages of development, it skipped several stages, reverting to an earlier stage and commencing its life cycle again. Following physical damage, the medusa would sink to the bottom of the tank, its tentacles would be re-absorbed and its body would assume a globular shape. From this ball of cells, growths or 'stolons' would appear, which would lengthen to become polyps. These polyps in turn would become free-floating medusae. It was as though a fully formed butterfly had reverted to its caterpillar stage. Biologists in the field were sceptical, so revolutionary was the change. However, the process was confirmed by another scientist, Stefan Piraino, but his paper was rejected by the journal *Nature.* Eventually, another publisher was found and the term 'immortal jellyfish' was coined. What was happening at a cellular level was that the jellyfish was undergoing a process of 'transdifferentiation'. Its cells were switching from one specialized cell line to another. This posed an intriguing question. If one cell was replaced by another, was the resulting organism a new organism or the same one? James Carlton, professor of marine sciences at Williams College, Massachusetts, argued that while the cells of this jellyfish were indeed immortal, the organism itself wasn't.[7]

As far as humans are concerned, if a muscle cell could be made to transdifferentiate into a brain cell, it would constitute a huge advancement and offer therapeutic solutions not available to us at present. As it is, human cells do sometimes spontaneously transdifferentiate but into cells we do not care for, namely cancer cells. Understanding the process of transdifferentiation better might lead us to new cancer treatments and even into the prevention of neoplasia.

Stem cells are one means we currently have of repairing or regenerating damaged or diseased tissue and are being used with success in treating conditions as diverse as multiple sclerosis and

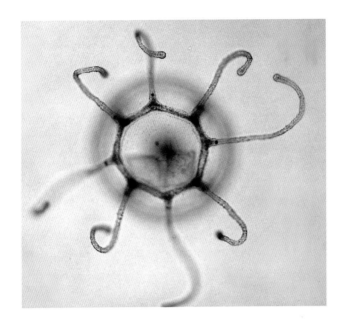

retinal macular degeneration. These stem cells are undifferentiated cells and again the pioneering work in stem cell research involved jellyfish, in this case the siphonophore *Crystalloides vitrea*. Ernst Haeckel, whose name has already emerged in connection with the biology and illustration of jellyfish, discovered that fragments removed from the embryos of this jellyfish went on to produce complete larvae. This was the first time the pluripotency of embryonic cells, viz. their ability to give rise to several different cell types, had been demonstrated and led to pioneering work on early embryo development by Wilhelm Roux and Hans Driesch.[8]

We use the term 'transdifferentiation' where an already differentiated cell becomes another differentiated cell. The process doesn't require the middle step of becoming a stem cell. *Turritopsis*, because it displays transdifferentiation, offers the possibility of skipping the stem cell stage and of moving directly from one cell type to another. As well as offering a better understanding of tissue repair, *Turritopsis* also tempts us with the prospect of being able to defy death. Professor Shin Kubota of the University of Kyoto's marine laboratory believes this small jellyfish holds the answer to immortality,[9] but here it is necessary to be reminded of the fate of Prince Tithonus.

Eos, the goddess of dawn, fell in love with Tithonus, a handsome Trojan prince. According to the Homeric *Hymn to Aphrodite*, Eos asked Zeus to grant Tithonus eternal life so that she could be with him for ever. She forgot, however, to ask for eternal youth and, as he lost his good looks, so she lost interest in him.

Immortality isn't without its problems. As Richard Holloway points out in his reflections on old age, the 'anti-ageing and

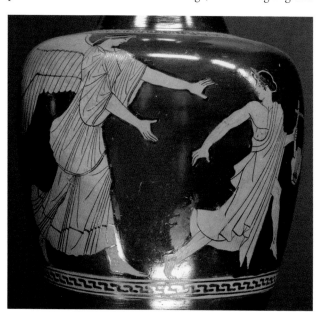

Greek vase
showing Eos
pursuing Tithonus,
c. 470 BC.

postponement of death' industry, acronymized as AAPD, has never been healthier.[10] Much time and effort is spent prolonging life, but scant attention is paid to the quality of that life. Few of us, I suspect, want to eke out an existence if there is the prospect of significant pain or disability. We do not want to share with Tithonus eternal life. What we really want is the blessing of eternal youth and the ability to re-grow the parts of us that have become damaged.

Meanwhile, Professor Kubota continues his research on jellyfish, growing generation after generation of *Turritopsis* in the laboratory. Using fine metal needles, he stabs the medusa several times to induce the process of transdifferentiation. Over a two-year period he has been able to witness regeneration many times at intervals as short as a month. He has also found that under two circumstances, during starvation and in cold conditions, the process of transdifferentiation is inhibited. Not content with experimenting with his 'immortal jellyfish', Professor Kubota is also keen to promulgate his message on television and on radio. An accomplished songwriter and performer, he has achieved star status with his songs about immortality. Wearing a red rubber hat sprouting tentacles, red sunglasses and a pair of red gloves, he croons into the microphone songs such as 'The Life Forever' and the 'Die-hard Medusa' to the delight of his Japanese audience.[11]

Jellyfish pop up frequently in other contexts, particularly in the biotechnology field. The search for bioactive compounds from marine animals has in the past yielded several of clinical importance. Jellyfish, because of their ability to produce toxic proteins in the form of venom, are obvious candidates for study. The box jellyfish known as the sea wasp, *Chironex fleckeri*, widely regarded as one of the most – if not *the* most – venomous animals, is a promising example but poses problems for researchers. How can significant amounts of venom be extracted when it comes as tiny packages lodged within nematocysts? Alcohol has been found to make nematocysts fire and with it box jellyfish can be 'milked' of their venom in reasonable amounts. The extract has been researched with the aim of developing drugs of potential benefit to us as well as antidotes to the venom. Research is also going on to isolate chemical compounds from jellyfish that might be of use in treating neurodegenerative diseases in humans, though claims that extracts from jellyfish improve memory and cognitive skills have as yet proved false. The history of isolating drugs that are useful to humans from animal venom has so far, with few exceptions, yielded disappointing results, but the potential for a significant breakthrough exists.

Jellyfish can also be of use to us in another respect, again to do with tissue healing. There is a well-established market for extracting collagen from animals as varied as pigs, cows and fish, but these sources risk contamination from viruses and prions. Collagen extracted from jellyfish carries less risk of contamination than existing animal sources and therefore has the potential to be used in tissue culture and in medicine. For example, it has been shown that dressings made from collagen extracted from the mesoglea of the barrel jellyfish, *Rhizostoma pulmo*, can actually speed up the healing process. Here there is an obvious clinical application where chronic ulceration exists of the sort that can lead to gangrene and often amputation. The collagen could provide the necessary scaffolding around which new tissue can grow.[12]

Few, I suspect, have heard of the contribution jellyfish have made to our understanding of the effects of microgravity on the human body. Spacecraft orbiting the earth create an environment in which objects, including human beings, appear weightless, but this has its problems, particularly when it comes to balance. In 1992, over 2,000 polyps of the moon jellyfish, *Aurelia aurita*, were included in the payload of the space shuttle *Columbia*. Dr Dorothy Spangenberg of the Eastern Virginia Medical School led a team whose purpose was to learn how microgravity influenced the development of *Aurelia* and see how weightlessness affected the gravity sensors, the statoliths, inside. Since statoliths contain crystals of calcium that resemble those found in the inner ear of humans, what happens in jellyfish ought to mimic what happens in us. What the nine-day mission showed was that as the ephyrae grew and matured into adult jellyfish back on earth, they lacked some of the gravity-sensing capabilities of their earthly counterparts. The crystals of calcium had failed to develop properly, suggesting that in humans too there could be a problem if the astronaut is subjected to prolonged periods of weightlessness in space, such as in a space station.[13] More research is needed, but it is important to remember that jellyfish provided the experimental material.

I began this chapter by implying that we should not be blinkered in our attitudes to creatures, particularly those that may cause us harm. As we have seen, they can provide us with chemicals that

An illustration of a rhizostomatid jellyfish from H.-M. Ducrotay Blainville's *Manuel d'actinologie ou de zoophytologie* (1834).

are beneficial, act as experimental animals in the investigation of human disease, and teach us about our own bodily functioning. Jellyfish, in particular, show us how animals remote from us on an evolutionary scale can nevertheless be useful in ways that could not have been envisaged even fifty years ago. Is it not unreasonable to suppose they have more to teach us yet?

7 World Domination

Yea, slimy things did crawl with legs upon the slimy sea.
Samuel Taylor Coleridge, *The Rime of the Ancient Mariner*

Jeremy Jackson, director of the Scripps Center for Marine Bio-diversity and Conservation in San Diego, claims that the health of the oceans is in a downward spiral. The ocean, a once complex system, he says, is being transformed into a much simpler one dominated by, among other things, jellyfish.[1] This transformation he labels 'the rise of slime'. In her book *Stung! On Jellyfish Blooms and the Future of the Ocean*, Lisa-ann Gershwin, director of the Australian Marine Stinger Advisory Services, acknowledges he could be right. 'It might seem outlandish and farcical that jelly-fish could rule the sea. But they've done it before, and now we have opened the door for them to do it again.'[2] Jellyfish blooms, she argues, are the outward, most visible part of a distressed ocean. The ecological balance has been disrupted because of multiple stressors, and opportunists like jellyfish are assuming increasing importance, displacing fish and other predators to become themselves 'top predator' in the sea.

It is a hotly debated and controversial area of research in which there are several interconnected issues. First is the state of the oceans. If they are truly in decline, what is it about jellyfish that favours them over other predators? Second, will a rise in jellyfish numbers be sufficient for them to assume a dominant role in the ocean ecosystem? Third, do we know enough about the ecology of different jellyfish, what causes some to bloom and others to

disappear, and is there enough reliable information available about jellyfish numbers to make sound predictions?

A swarm of moon jellyfish, sometimes likened to oil slicks offshore. Their sting is mostly harmless to humans.

The health of the oceans is certainly topical and our knowledge of what goes on in the ocean food web is expanding all the time. Professor Alex Rogers from the University of Oxford leads an initiative known as IPSO (International Programme on the State of the Ocean), which warns of multiple threats to our oceans. He argues that conditions are ripe for a mass extinction event, similar to ones that affected our seas in the distant past. In 2013 IPSO published its State of the Ocean report, which drew a number of conclusions.[3] While acknowledging that oceans shielded us from the worst effects of climate change by absorbing excess carbon dioxide and heat from the atmosphere, more recently there has been a warming and acidification of the sea and, in consequence, lower oxygen concentrations in the water. The result of these processes can be seen in the bleaching of coral in places like the Great Barrier Reef, the melting of the Greenland ice sheet and a destabilization of food webs in the ocean. Other stressors were thought to play a part too, such as humans taking too many fish from the sea and polluting it with waste, from agro-chemicals to microplastics. The resilience of the oceans to climate change, it is argued, is being seriously compromised and much of this has to do with the actions of humanity. This being the case, there is little room for complacency and action needs to be taken now.

The second issue is what it is about jellyfish, in particular, that allows them to exploit such an ecosystem under stress. First, jellyfish appear to tolerate low oxygen concentrations in seawater far better than creatures with higher metabolic demands, such as fish and mammals. Second, there is some evidence to suggest a rise in sea temperature causes at least some jellyfish to actually increase their reproductive rates and lengthen their reproductive season. Third, jellyfish can go without food for a considerable time, becoming smaller in the process but no less active in a reproductive sense than their better-fed cousins. When the food supply does increase, so does the size of the jellyfish. This allows them to survive periods of food shortage, a situation which isn't the case for many other marine creatures. Fourth, while jellyfish can be voracious feeders, denuding the sea of eggs, larvae and small invertebrates, they have relatively few predators.

From this it would appear that jellyfish are well placed to exploit situations in which their competitors fail. They show a greater adaptability to changing circumstances and, while their body design doesn't enable them to actively pursue their prey, nevertheless, as passive drifters in the water, they show themselves to be voracious feeders and capable of withstanding food shortages. As Gershwin points out, they have spent over 600 million years perfecting the art of survival. Evolution has seen to it that they are well placed to exploit the changes in the marine environment outlined by ipso. Whether they will ever assume a dominant role in the ocean is a much more contentious issue and it is here that our knowledge of the numbers and habits of particular jellyfish comes into play.

Jellyfish numbers can vary considerably. Swarms of jellyfish have invaded seawater-cooling systems and have even paralysed an American nuclear-powered aircraft carrier, the uss *Ronald Reagan*. Salmon farms as far apart as Scotland and Chile have been put out of business because of swarms of jellyfish, and the tourist industry in Australia has repeatedly suffered from invasions of box jellyfish, putting a halt to bathing in coastal resorts like Queensland. On one dramatic night in the Philippines, power was lost in the capital city Manila, sparking fears of a military coup. In fact the outage had been caused by jellyfish, a swarm of which had been sucked into the cooling pipes of the main power plant.[4] Such is the power of swarms of jellyfish that attention is now being focused on their habits and ways of preventing or ameliorating their impact.

Our understanding of what causes a bloom in any one species of jellyfish is still embryonic. A bloom can be part of the normal growth cycle of a jellyfish, a seasonal event. Records extending back to 1785 concerning the numbers of the mauve stinger jellyfish *Pelagia noctiluca* in the western Mediterranean have indicated that major blooms there tend to occur every twelve years.[5] Climatic factors such as high temperatures and atmospheric pressures, together with low rainfall, appear to favour an explosion in numbers of this species of jellyfish. Ironically, they are the same factors that encourage excellent vintages among the vines of southern France. Knowledge of what precipitates blooms in other species of jellyfish varies from incomplete to nothing at all. Their ability to dramatically increase is not confined to cnidarian jellyfish, but is a feature of comb jellies too. The story of two comb jellies, *Mnemiopsis leidyi* and *Beroe ovata*, serves as an illustration of what can happen to jellyfish numbers.[6]

The Black Sea has always been a polluted body of water, draining as it does several rivers that run through industrial areas serving millions of people in several countries. It has 'dead zones', which are areas of low oxygen concentration, the result of excessive nutrient pollution, usually from human activity. Despite this, it has been intensively fished. *Mnemiopsis* was accidentally transported to the Black Sea, probably in a ship's ballast tank, all the way from the Gulf of Mexico. This comb jelly had never been recorded in the Black Sea before. The conditions proved ideal for it to exploit. Fish stocks were already on the decline and the whole ecosystem was under stress, so *Mnemiopsis* found itself with few predators. The result was an explosion in its numbers, assisted by the fact that this particular jellyfish was a fecund, self-fertilizing hermaphrodite. Add to this its ability to quickly repair and regenerate itself and the invasion became a plague. Commercial fishing for anchovies was brought to a standstill. The population of *Mnemiopsis* peaked in around 1989.

Eight years later, another comb jelly, *Beroe ovata*, was also noted to be present in the Black Sea. This jellyfish had, like *Mnemiopsis*, been accidentally introduced, but this one was a known predator on *Mnemiopsis*. *Beroe* proved to be very effective in controlling the numbers of *Mnemiopsis*. As *Mnemiopsis* numbers declined, so did those of *Beroe*, and as a result of the reduction in comb jellies in the Black Sea, fish stocks started to rise. The system had righted itself!

Unfortunately, one cannot rely on self-correcting systems in nature to deal with blooms brought about by man-made changes

The mauve stinger, *Pelagia noctiluca*, seen in growing numbers on Mediterranean beaches.

to the ecosystem. After what happened in the Black Sea, it was decided to introduce *Beroe* into the Caspian Sea following the arrival there of large numbers of *Mnemiopsis*. Disappointingly, the same self-correcting process failed to operate. The numbers of jellyfish remained high and zooplankton stocks low.

Previously, in Chesapeake Bay in North America, the sea nettle *Chrysaora quinquecirrha* had proved a considerable nuisance with

its summer and autumn blooms. Fishing and tourism had been impacted and jellyfish densities had reached an average of sixteen individuals for every cubic metre of seawater. Various strategies had been tried to reduce their numbers, ranging from chemicals to sound waves to biological control with a predatory sea slug. None proved effective.[7]

The search for a better understanding of what triggers blooms and what might bring them under control has proved frustrating. Attention has focused on the life history of particular jellyfish and the role played both by polyps and medusae. Strobilation, or the budding of young medusae from the polyp precursor, is thought to be governed by several environmental factors, one being temperature, others the degree of salinity and light exposure. Unfortunately, the exact trigger can vary within a single species, depending on where it is found. The moon jellyfish, *Aurelia aurita*, for example, produces juvenile medusae in February after a prolonged cold period in Kertinge Nor Fjord in Denmark, while the very same species undergoes strobilation in Gullmar Fjord in western Sweden in October. Likewise, *Chrysaora chesapeakei* in Chesapeake Bay produces ephyrae in late spring and summer, while its near relative *Cyanea capillata* from the same area favours autumn. We now know that the trace element iodine is important in strobilation and that even the human hormone thyroxine can influence the process, though the precise biochemical processes involved are not understood.[8]

Lisa-ann Gershwin claims in her book that around the world we are witnessing jellyfish blooms more often, and that they are bigger in geographical coverage and longer in seasonal duration.[9] Her prognostication that these creatures may again rule the seas remains a distinct possibility and her argument that they may be well placed to exploit adverse conditions in the oceans is a cogent one. Other scientists, however, are more cautious in their

A jellyfish bloom from *Cassell's Natural History* (1881).

predictions.[10] They point out a lack of consensus as to whether 'gelatinous zooplankton' have increased from historical levels and argue that not enough is known about jellyfish numbers to be confident about distinguishing natural fluctuations from long-term population changes. Steven Haddock points out that jellyfish have been 'blooming and busting in the oceans for millions of years' and that the present increase in numbers of many species of jellyfish may simply represent a natural cycle. Two other authorities, Kylie Pitt and Cathy Lucas, emphasize that two meta-analyses of data relating to numbers have come to opposite conclusions.[11] The U.S. National Center for Ecological Analysis and Synthesis (NCEAS) has convened a working group to examine the data we already have. They too conclude that there is currently not enough reliable long-term information to say for sure that there has been a significant rise in jellyfish numbers in recent years. Natural fluctuations in jellyfish populations over time need to be factored in. For example, some parts of the world such as the Bering Sea, which provided reliable evidence that jellyfish numbers were expanding, subsequently showed a decline in numbers.[12]

There is a further factor to consider. Blooms are regarded as 'notable events' and therefore worthy of press coverage, while an apparent absence of jellyfish in the sea isn't newsworthy. This contributes to a false overall perception of jellyfish numbers. A global database, compiled from a variety of sources, would go some way to solving the problem and to address this a Jellyfish Database Initiative (JEDI) has been set up.[13] There is also a website where the public can report jellyfish sightings (jellywatch.org). It is to be hoped that more information will allow more accurate estimates of jellyfish abundance in the future.

It is perhaps worth mentioning one other complicating matter in regard to making links between jellyfish numbers and

A Jellyfish Like the Moon: Japanese scroll painting by Nagasawa Rosetsu (1754–1799).

Mnemiopsis leidyi, the warty comb jelly that invaded the Black Sea.

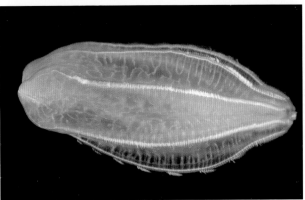

Beroe ovata, a comb jelly that saw off *Mnemiopsis* from the Black Sea.

Pl. XI.

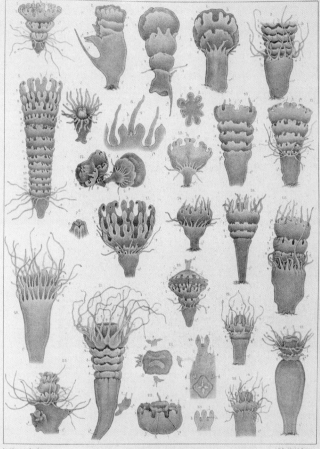

STROBILA OF AURELIA FLAVIDULA.

changes in the ocean environment, and that is our tendency to demonize jellyfish. Instead of blaming jellyfish for a deteriorating ocean ecosystem, the finger of blame ought really to point at humans themselves. Our continued abuse of the oceans is resulting in a situation where fish and other marine creatures fail and where jellyfish are perceived as winners. As one commentator, Karl Mathiesen, put it, 'Jellyfish thrive on the environmental chaos humans create.'[14] It can also be argued that a disproportionate amount of attention is given to the potentially harmful aspects of the jellyfish, while their benefits are being ignored, something I alluded to in the last chapter. Thomas Doyle and others suggest that the narrative about jellyfish is certainly not one of doom and gloom. They point out that an important function provided by jellyfish is to act as a sink for greenhouse gases through the sequestration of carbon. As a result of jellyfish carcasses accumulating on the seabed, transfer of carbon from the surface waters to the seabed is actually facilitated.[15] The role of jellyfish in recycling nutrients is another beneficial function. Professor Pitt shows in one study that jellyfish blooms in Lake Illawarra in Australia produce up to 8 per cent of the nitrogen requirements of the phytoplankton there.[16] As a result of swimming between different layers of a column of water, jellyfish also facilitate the transport of nutrients and encourage their dispersion to areas that are relatively depleted in nutrients. It must also be remembered that jellyfish form a source of food for a variety of marine creatures, from sea turtles to certain species of fish, some of which are commercially valuable. A team from Heriot-Watt University in Edinburgh found, to their surprise, that the Norway lobster, worth £78 million to the Scottish fishing industry alone, eats the carcasses of jellyfish, scaring other scavengers away in order to gorge on the jellyfish remains.[17] Penguins too, it seems, turn to jellyfish for sustenance, along with albatrosses and the larvae

Sonrel's illustration of strobilation in the moon jellyfish, from Agassiz's *Contributions to the Natural History of the United States of America* (1857).

A stranding of the bluebottle jellyfish, otherwise known as the Portuguese man-of-war. Armadas reached Queensland beaches in 2019, stinging thousands of beachgoers.

of eels. The best-known consumer of all is the leatherback sea turtle, *Dermochelys coriacea*. A large predator itself, weighing approximately 450 kg (1,000 lb), one turtle can consume three-quarters of its own body mass in a single day. It eats primarily jellyfish and has two sharply pointed cusps, one on its upper jaw, the other on its lower, which enable it to pierce and hold on to jellyfish. It also boasts backwards-pointing spines lining its digestive tract from its mouth through to its stomach, which help break down jellyfish quickly. Unfortunately, a turtle can easily confuse its prey with a floating polythene bag, a mistake that can prove lethal. It would seem that many more animals than was previously thought rely on jellyfish as a source of food, forcing a rethink of the importance of jellyfish ecology in understanding the ocean web. New techniques, from chemical signatures to analysing stomach contents for jellyfish DNA, to physically mounting cameras onto marine animals, have overturned the view that, because jellyfish are mainly water and low in calories, they are ignored by ocean predators. In the final analysis, the benefits and disadvantages of jellyfish to mankind could prove equal.

How then should we regard these creatures? As creatures to be feared, animals aspiring to be a dominant force in the oceans, displacing fish and serving as a threat to humanity itself? As an early evolutionary experiment that informs us about evolution and provides us with products that are useful to us? Or simply as beautiful creatures perfectly adapted to their watery world and entitled to their place in the food web? Opinions will of course vary and, over the course of time, as more is known about them, those opinions are likely to change. My suspicion is that jellyfish will always be relegated to the fringe of the animal world and will remain objects of suspicion. Largely out of sight, difficult to study, inclined to be prolific and therefore dispensable, they will, I sense, continue to be seen as alien beings, convenient

A leatherback turtle. They can mistake plastic bags for jellyfish with fatal consequences.

145

The flower-hat
jellyfish, *Olindias
formosus*, with its
fluorescent-tipped
tentacles, must
rank as one of the
most attractive
animals in the sea.

receptacles for our negative feelings about what is wrong with
the state of the oceans. Killian Quigley from the Environmental
Institute in Sydney draws our attention to one recent initiative
that aspires to use jellyfish, in particular their mucus, as a means
of removing microplastics from the ocean. As he points out, it
is as though one unwanted item has been enlisted to remove
another, addressing with a single approach what are perceived as
two environmental problems. He goes on to say: 'It's an astound-
ing alignment. What does it say about language and about
imagination, that it is possible to couple living organisms and
minuscule rubbish in this way – to conjoin them, rhetorically
and literally, as an unsavoury pair in need of cleaning up?'[18]

It is clear that the time has come to re-examine our attitudes
to jellyfish and to be wary of attempts to demonize them. Instead
we should aim to come to some sort of accommodation. They
matter, and whether we like it or not they are not going to disappear from the oceans and are entitled to their place in the
natural world.

In an article on why birds matter, Jonathan Franzen says this:

The radical otherness of birds is integral to their beauty and value. They are always among us but never of us. Their indifference to us ought to serve as a chastening reminder that we are not the measure of all things . . . birds live squarely in the present . . . their world is very much alive.[19]

Much the same could be said of jellyfish, which have inhabited the earth much longer than birds and, for that matter, than *Homo sapiens.* Jellyfish, like birds, are here for the long haul and, at the very least, deserve our respect.

Timeline of the Jellyfish

4TH CENTURY BC	1ST CENTURY AD	1560	1671
Aristotle names jellyfish 'Acalephs' but is uncertain whether they are plants or animals	Pliny the Elder draws attention to a light-emitting jellyfish, *Pulmo marinus*	Conrad Gessner includes an illustration of a jellyfish in his *Historia animalium*	Friderich Martens records the first comb jelly near Spitsbergen

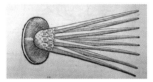 

1812	1835	1840	1849
Georges Cuvier creates the group 'Radiata', which includes jellyfish	Christian Ehrenberg draws attention to the anatomical complexity of jellyfish	Michael Sars discovers the life cycle of *Aurelia aurita*	Thomas Henry Huxley publishes his paper on the anatomy and affinities of the Medusae

1913	1988	1989	1992
Charles Richet and Paul Portier are awarded the Nobel Prize for discovering anaphylaxis as a result of research on venom from *Physalia*	Christian Sommer notes that a jellyfish called *Turritopsis* appears to age in reverse	The comb jelly *Mnemiopsis* brings commercial fishing for anchovies to a halt in the Black Sea	Ephyrae of *Aurelia aurita* are included in the payload of space shuttle *Columbia*

| 1723 | 1744 | 1752 | 1809 |

Jean-André Peyssonnel establishes the animal nature of coral

Abraham Trembley investigates the polyp *Hydra* and draws attention to its animal nature

Carl Linnaeus allocates jellyfish to the group 'zoophytes' and gives them the alternative name 'medusa'

François Péron and Charles-Alexandre Lésueur publish their account of jellyfish collected on Baudin's expedition to Terra Australis

| 1860 | 1879 | 1880 | 1904 |

Louis Agassiz's *Contributions to the Natural History of the United States of America* is largely devoted to jellyfish

Ernst Haeckel's monograph on siphonophores collected during the *Challenger* expedition is published

Ray Lankester describes the first freshwater jellyfish

Ernst Haeckel publishes *Kunstformen der Natur* with its plates of jellyfish

| 1997 | 2008 | 2013 |

Members of the Scyphozoa, Cubozoa and Hydrozoa are grouped together as 'Medusozoa' because a medusa phase is present in all three

The Nobel Prize in Chemistry is awarded to Osamu Shimomura, Martin Chalfie and Roger Tsien for the discovery and development of green fluorescent protein from the jellyfish *Aequorea victoria*

Lisa-ann Gershwin warns that marine ecosystems are in free fall and jellyfish blooms are increasing

SIMPLE CLASSIFICATION OF JELLYFISH

PHYLUM CNIDARIA

PHYLUM CTENOPHORA

SCYPHOZOA

'True' jellyfish

HYDROZOA

Siphonophores
Other colonial and
non-colonial hydrozoans

CUBOZOA

Box jellyfish

CTENOPHORA

Comb jellies

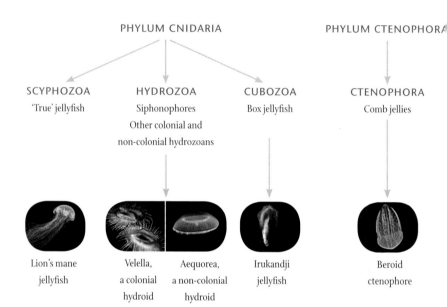

Lion's mane
jellyfish

Velella,
a colonial
hydroid

Aequorea,
a non-colonial
hydroid

Irukandji
jellyfish

Beroid
ctenophore

Appendix 1: A Brief Description of Individual Species of Jellyfish Mentioned in the Text

Barrel jellyfish or dustbin lid jellyfish, Rhizostoma pulmo
The solid spherical bell, measuring up to 40 cm (16 in.) across (occasionally more), lacks marginal tentacles. The umbrella margin instead has lappets. The colouring tends to be variable. It has a large manubrium and four pairs of large frilly oral arms. The sting is weak.

Blue jellyfish, Cyanea lamarckii
Similar to *capillata* but smaller, with a bell up to 15 cm (6 in.) in diameter and tentacles up to 1 m (3 ft) long. Its sting is less severe than that of *capillata* and, despite its name, it is frequently white rather than blue.

Compass jellyfish, Chrysaora hysoscella
The bell is saucer-shaped and up to 30 cm (12 in.) in diameter. Its 24 tentacles are arranged in eight groups of three. It is yellowish-white in colour with sixteen characteristic V-shaped brown markings radiating from the centre of the bell. A long, slender manubrium leads to four oral arms. It can give a painful sting resulting in weals on the skin. It changes sex from male to female as it matures.

Helmet jellyfish, Periphylla periphylla

A deep-sea jellyfish, bell-shaped and up to 30 cm (12 in.) across. It has twelve stiff tentacles and is red in colour. Widely distributed and particularly abundant in some Norwegian fjords. Bioluminescent.

Lion's mane jellyfish, Cyanea capillata

The large bell has been known to reach 2 m (6½ ft) in diameter, making it one of the largest jellyfish worldwide. It has a reddish-brown colour and the tentacles, which arise under the bell rather than from its edge, are long and hair-like, reaching up to 37 m (120 ft) in length. The oral arms are short and frilly. The bell is scalloped into eight lappets. It tends to be found close to the water's surface. The sting is painful but rarely fatal. It is found worldwide.

Moon jellyfish, Aurelia aurita

The translucent, umbrella-shaped bell, measuring up to 40 cm (16 in.) across, bears short, hair-like tentacles. Its manubrium has four short arms. Characteristically, there are four purple, horseshoe-shaped gonads, which are visible through the surface of the bell. The genus *Aurelia* has a wide distribution worldwide and is frequently found in estuaries and harbours. Its sting tends to be mild, though occasionally it can result in local pain and skin weals.

Nomura's jellyfish, Nemopilema nomurai

Huge, with a bell up to 2 m (6½ ft) across. Numerous mouths lie beneath the bell. A voracious feeder and a threat to the fishing industry in the sea between Japan and China.

Mauve stinger, Pelagia noctiluca
The warty, mushroom-shaped bell, up to 10 cm (4 in.) across, bears eight thin tentacles. The colour is variable from purple to brownish-red. The bell is covered with pink or mauve warts bearing stinging cells. The manubrium bears four frilly oral arms. It has no polyp stage in its life cycle. It is widely distributed and common in the Mediterranean. As its name suggests, it is bioluminescent and leaves a luminous mucus behind when handled. It delivers a painful sting.

Upside-down jellyfish, Cassiopea xamachana
The flattened bell, measuring up to 30 cm (12 in.) across, normally lies on the seabed, though the animal is capable of swimming. The edges of its eight oral arms are fused and bear numerous frilly extensions. These incorporate symbiotic algae, which supply most of the animal's nutrition through photosynthesis. Rather than having a central mouth, each extension has its own mouth. Found in warm tropical seas.

HYDROZOANS

Crystal jellyfish, Aequorea victoria
The transparent bell measures up to 8 cm (3 in.) across and bears numerous tentacles at its margin. Found off the west coast of North America and the source of aequorin and green fluorescent protein.

Freshwater jellyfish, Craspedacusta sowerbii
A delicate, translucent freshwater jellyfish measuring 2 cm (¾ in.) in diameter with numerous tentacles at its margin. Native to the Yangtze basin in China but with a worldwide distribution. In cold winter months its polyp phase can undergo dormancy as podocysts.

'Immortal' jellyfish, Turritopsis dohrnii

As tall as it is wide with a bell the size of a fingernail, it is transparent but for a bright red stomach. Numerous small tentacles arise from the bell margin. Found in the Mediterranean and off the coast of Japan.

BOX JELLYFISH

Carybdea sivickisi

A small box jellyfish measuring 1 cm (⅓ in.) across its bell and bearing four tentacles. Found in shallow waters in the Pacific. Notable for its mating behaviour and internal fertilization.

Irukandji jellyfish, Carukia barnesi

The square, 2.5 cm (1 in.) diameter bell has, arising from each corner, four contractile tentacles which, when fully extended, can reach 50 cm (20 in.) in length. Found off the coast of Northern Australia, usually in deeper waters. An agile swimmer. Its sting can be lethal.

Sea wasp, Chironex fleckeri

The largest box jellyfish and the most lethal. The bell measures up to 30 cm (12 in.) across and has groups of retractile tentacles up to 3 m (10 ft) in length arising from its four corners. Transparent, with a pale blue colour. Found in the coastal waters of Australia, New Guinea, the Philippines and Vietnam. As it grows it becomes more of an active hunter.

COLONIAL HYDROID POLYP

By-the-wind-sailor, Velella velella

A highly individual hydroid polyp measuring up to 10 cm (4 in.) in length, having a deep blue colour. Short tentacles hang from a float that bears a semicircular sail. In the western hemisphere the sail, situated on a diagonal to the long axis of the body, runs from northeast to southwest. In specimens found on northeast Pacific beaches the sail is set in the direction of northwest to southeast. In other words, *Velella* exists as two types in the positioning of its sail. It can cause skin irritation when handled and, on occasions, can be found in large numbers washed up on beaches. Widely distributed worldwide.

COLONIAL SIPHONOPHORES (HYDROZOANS)

Giant siphonophore, Praya dubia

A deep-sea hydrozoan with a thin body up to 50 m (164 ft) long composed of zooids. An active swimmer found in deep sea. Widespread globally.

Portuguese man-of-war, Physalia physalis

A colonial hydroid and a siphonophore, so named because of its resemblance to an eighteenth-century Portuguese armed ship. The gas-filled bladder acts as a float and bears a crest. Tinged blue, it measures up to 30 cm (12 in.) in length and bears retractile tentacles that can reach many metres below the water surface and which have a beaded appearance. The beads bear stinging cells that can inflict a powerful sting even after the animal is beached. Found in the Atlantic, Indian and Pacific oceans.

Beroe cucumis

A comb jelly in the shape of a sac up to 15 cm (6 in.) in length. Transparent, with eight longitudinal combs made up of plates of hairs that beat to produce a shimmering effect. There are no tentacles and a large mouth is used to engulf prey, usually other comb jellies such as *Bolinopsis*. Originally native to the Western Atlantic. Spread to the Black Sea and subsequently to the Caspian Sea, North Sea and Baltic.

Bolinopsis infundibulum

Like Beroe, transparent and of similar shape and size, again with eight longitudinal rows of combs, but having additionally two small tentacles bearing fringes. The mouth is surrounded by two large, mucus-covered flaps. It feeds on zooplankton. Widespread from the North Atlantic to the Mediterranean.

Sea gooseberry, Pleurobrachia pileus

Small (up to 2.5 cm/1 in.), transparent comb jelly with an oval or spherical shape, bearing eight combs as well as tentacles up to 50 cm (20 in.) in length which are retractile. Feeds chiefly on copepods. Found in the North and South Atlantic, North Sea, Baltic, Mediterranean and the Black Sea.

Appendix 2:
Where to See Jellyfish in Captivity

UK

The Deep, Tower Street, Hull, HU1 4DP

National Sea Life Centre, The Water's Edge, Brinkley Place, Birmingham, B1 2HL

Sea Life Blackpool, Promenade, Blackpool, FY1 5AA

Sea Life Great Yarmouth, Marine Parade, Great Yarmouth, Norfolk, NR30 3AH

Sea Life London Aquarium, County Hall, Westminster Bridge Road, London, SE1 7PB

Scarborough Sea Life Sanctuary, Scalby Mills, Scarborough, YO12 6RP

Weymouth Sea Life Adventure Park, Lodmoor Country Park, Weymouth, DT4 7SX

USA

Birch Aquarium, Scripps Institution of Oceanography, 2300, Expedition Way, La Jolle, CA 92037

National Aquarium, 501 E Pratt Street, Baltimore, MD 21202

New England Aquarium, 1 Central Wharf, Boston, MA 02110

Monterey Bay Aquarium, 886, Cannery Row, Monterey, CA 93940

Seattle Aquarium, 1483 Alaskan Way, Pier 59, Seattle, WA 98101

Shedd Aquarium, 1200 S Lake Shore Drive, Chicago, IL 60605

CANADA

Ripley's Aquarium, 288 Bremner Boulevard, Toronto, ON, MSV 3L9

Vancouver Aquarium, 845 Avison Way, Vancouver, BC, V6G 3E2

JAPAN

Kamo Aquarium, 636 Okubo, Imaizumi, Tsuruoka City, Japan

AUSTRALIA

Sea World Gold Coast, Seaworld Drive, Main Beach, QLD 4217

SINGAPORE

Sea Aquarium, 8 Sentosa Gateway, Sentosa Island

HONG KONG

Ocean Park Jellyfish Aquarium, 180 Wong Chuck Hang Road, Aberdeen

PHILIPPINES

Manila Ocean Park, Manila, Luzon 1000

CHINA

Royal Ocean World, No. 3 Gaoyang Rd, Fushun 113008

References

INTRODUCTION

1 Matt Wilkinson, *Restless Creatures: The Story of Life in Ten Movements* (London, 2016), p. 161.
2 Jean Sprackland, *Strands* (London, 2012), p. 38.
3 Tom Fort, *The Book of Eels* (London, 2002), p. xi.
4 Xi-Ping Dong et al., 'Embryos, Polyps and Medusae of the Early Cambrian Scyphozoan, *Olovooides*', *Proceedings of the Royal Society B: Biological Sciences*, CCLXXX/1757 (2013).
5 Feng Tang et al., '*Eoandromeda* and the Origin of Ctenophora', *Evolution and Development*, XIII/5 (2011), pp. 408–14.
6 Kenneth M. Halanych, 'The Ctenophores Lineage is Older than Sponges? That Cannot be Right! Or Can It?', *Journal of Experimental Biology*, 218 (2015), pp. 592–7.

1 A LINEAGE OF UNCERTAINTY

1 Aristotle, *History of Animals*, trans. A. L. Peck (Cambridge, MA, 1979).
2 Susannah Gibson, *Animal, Vegetable, Mineral? How Eighteenth-century Science Disrupted the Natural Order* (Oxford, 2015).
3 Georges-Louis Leclerc, comte de Buffon, *Histoire Naturelle*, trans. William Smellie (London, 1785).
4 Oliver Goldsmith, *Animated Nature* (Liverpool, 1810), vol. IV, pp. 307–9.
5 Gibson, *Animal, Vegetable, Mineral?*, pp. 120–28.

6 Sylvia and Howard Lenhoff, *Hydra and the Birth of Experimental Biology: 1744, Abraham Trembley's Mémoires Concerning the Polyps* (Pacific Grove, CA, 1986).

7 Mary P. Winsor, *Starfish, Jellyfish and the Order of Life* (New Haven, CT, and London, 1976), p. 15.

8 François Péron, *Voyage de découvertes aux terres australes* (Paris, 1815).

9 Winsor, *Starfish, Jellyfish*, pp. 28–43.

10 Ibid., pp. 44–73.

11 Personal communication with Mary Winsor re: the difference between Cuvier and Agassiz, February 2018.

12 Louis Agassiz, *Contributions to the Natural History of the United States of America*, vol. IV (Boston, MA, 1862), pp. 88–9.

13 Christoph Irmscher, *Louis Agassiz: Creator of American Science* (Boston, MA, 2013), p. 129.

14 Michael Anctil, *The Dawn of the Neuron: The Early Struggle to Trace the Origins of Nervous Systems* (Quebec, 2015), pp. 35–55.

15 Thomas Henry Huxley, 'On the Anatomy and the Affinities of the Family of the Medusae', *Philosophical Transactions of the Royal Society of London*, 139 (London, 1849), pp. 415–34.

16 Ernst Haeckel, *Monographie der Médusen, Challenger Expedition, 1872–1876* (Jena, 1879–81).

17 Frederick S. Russell, 'Obituary of Dr Marie V. Lebour', *Journal of the Marine Biological Association UK*, 52 (1972), pp. 777–8.

18 Steven H. D. Haddock, 'A Golden Age of Gelata: Past and Future Research on Planktonic Ctenophores and Cnidarians', *Hydrobiologia*, DXXX/1–3 (2004), pp. 549–56.

19 Celeste Olalquiaga, 'François Péron and the Taxonomic Delicacies of the Jellyfish', *Cabinet Magazine*, 21 (2006), www.cabinetmagazine.org.

2 TOXIC BUT FASCINATING

1 *War of the Worlds*, see http://en.wikipedia.org, accessed December 2016.

2 *Arrival*, see http://en.wikipedia.org, accessed July 2017.

3 Rob Williams, 'Aliens Could Resemble Jellyfish the Size
of a Football Field says Government Advisor',
www.independent.co.uk, 6 July 2012.

4 Mahdokht Jouiaei et al., 'Ancient Venom Aystems: A Review
of Cnidarian Toxins', *Toxins*, 7 (2015), pp. 2251–70.

5 Personal communication with Bryan Fry, November 2018.

6 Chris Nickson, 'Jack Barnes and the Irukandji Enigma',
www.lifeinthefastlane.com, 21 November 2014.

7 Ovid, *Metamorphoses*, Book IV, trans. A. S. Kline (eBook,
1 January 2004), pp. 753–803.

8 Percy Bysshe Shelley, 'On the Medusa of Leonardo da Vinci',
in *Posthumous Poems by Percy Bysshe Shelley*, ed. Mary W. Shelley
(London, 1824).

9 Emma E. Davidson, 'The Painting Gianni Versace Commissioned
but Never Lived To See', www.dazeddigital.com, 17 January 2018.

10 Sylvia Plath, 'Medusa' [1962], in *Collected Poems* (London, 1981).

11 Sigmund Freud, 'Das Medusenhaupt' [1922], in Sigmund
Freud Papers (1859–85), Library of Congress, Washington, DC.

12 Marianne Moore, 'A Jellyfish' [1959], in *New Collected Poems
of Marianne Moore*, ed. Heather Cass White (London, 2017).

13 Michael Dawson, 'Five New Subspecies of *Mastigias* from
Marine Lakes in Palau, Micronesia', *Journal of the Marine
Biological Association UK*, LXXXV/3 (2005), pp. 679–94.

14 Brad J. Gemmell et al., 'Suction-based Propulsion as a Basis for
Efficient Animal Swimming', *Nature Communications*, VI/8790 (2015).

15 Sabrine Fossett et al., 'Current-orientated Swimming by
Jellyfish and its Role in Bloom Maintenance', *Current Biology*,
XXV/3 (2015).

16 Ravi D. Nath et al., 'The Jellyfish *Cassiopea* Exhibits a Sleep-like
State', *Current Biology*, XXVII/19 (2017).

17 Mike N. Dawson and Laura E. Martin, 'Migrations by *Mastigias*',
www2.eve.ucdavis.edu (2001).

18 Stein Kaartvedt et al., 'Social Behaviour in Mesopelagic Jellyfish',
Scientific Reports, V/11310 (2015).

19 David Albert, 'What's on the Mind of a Jellyfish? A Review of Behavioural Observations on *Aurelia sp.* Jellyfish', *Neuroscience and Biobehavioral Reviews*, xxxv/3 (2011), pp. 474–82.

20 Robert Macfarlane, *The Wild Places* (London, 2007).

3 FLOATS, EYES AND COMBS

1 Ray Lankester, 'On a New Jellyfish of the Order *Trachomedusae* Living in Freshwater', *Nature*, 22 (1880), pp. 147–8.

2 T. H. Huxley, 'Upon Animal Individuality', *Proceedings of the Royal Institution of Great Britain*, 11 (1852), pp. 184–9.

3 Stephen Jay Gould, 'A Most Ingenious Paradox', in *The Flamingo's Smile* (New York, 1985), pp. 78–95.

4 G. O. Mackie, 'Siphonophores, Bud Colonies and Super-organisms', in *The Lower Metazoa*, ed. Ellsworth C. Dougherty (Berkeley, CA, 1963), p. 336.

5 John Blaxter and Bruce Douglas, 'Siphonophore Biology', *Advances in Marine Biology*, xxiv (London, 1987).

6 S.H.D. Haddock et al., 'Bioluminescent and Red Fluorescent Lures in a Deep Sea Siphonophore', *Science*, xxxix/5732 (2005).

7 Jamie Seymour, 'Are we Using the Correct First Aid for Jellyfish?', *Medical Journal of Australia*, ccvi/6 (2017), pp. 249–50.

8 Dan-E Nilsson et al., 'Advanced Optics in a Jellyfish Eye', *Nature*, 435 (2005), pp. 201–5.

9 Cheryl Lewis Ames and Tristan A. F. Long, 'Courtship and Reproduction in *Carybdea sivickisi*', *Marine Biology*, cxlvii/2 (2005), pp. 477–83.

10 Lisa-ann Gershwin and P.J.F. Davie, 'A Remarkable New Jellyfish from Coastal Australia Representing a New Sub-order within the *Rhizostomeae*', *Memoirs of the Queensland Museum*, lvi/2 (2013), pp. 625–30.

11 Matt Simon, 'Absurd Creature of the Week: Don't You Dare Call the *Deepstaria* Jellyfish a Whale Placenta', www.wired.com/science, 13 November 2015.

12 Leonid L. Moroz, 'Convergent Evolution of Neural Systems in
    Ctenophores', *Journal of Experimental Biology*, CCXVIII/4 (2015),
    pp. 598–61.
13 Casey W. Dunn, Sally P. Leys and Steven H. D. Haddock, 'The
    Hidden Biology of Sponges and Ctenophores', *Trends in Ecology
    and Evolution*, XXX/5 (2015), pp. 282–91.

4 THE ILLUSTRATOR'S NIGHTMARE

1 Conrad Gessner, *Icones animalium* (1560), p. 198.
2 Ulisse Aldrovandi, *De reliquis animalibus exanguibus, De Zoophytis*,
    Lib. IV (Bologna, 1606), p. 575.
3 François Péron and Charles-Alexandre Lésueur,
    'Histoire générale et particulière de tous les animaux qui
    composent la famille des Méduses', *Annales du Muséum
    d'Histoire naturelle, Paris*, 14 (1809 and 1818), pp. 218–28 and
    325–66.
4 John West-Sooby, 'An Artist in the Making: The Early Drawings
    of Charles-Alexandre Lésueur during the Baudin Expedition
    to Australia', in *Framing French Culture*, ed. Natalie Edwards,
    Ben McCann and Peter Poiana (Adelaide, 2015).
5 Jacqueline Goy, 'François Péron, Charles-Alexandre Lésueur and
    the First Classification of Medusae', *Archives of Natural History*,
    XIX/3 (1992), pp. 401–5.
6 Christoph Irmscher, *Louis Agassiz: Creator of American Science*
    (Boston, MA, 2013), p. 162.
7 Ernst Haeckel, *Das System der Medusen* (London, 2018).
8 Robert J. Richards, *The Tragic Sense of Life: Ernst Haeckel and
    the Struggle Over Evolutionary Thought* (Chicago, IL, 2008).
9 Susan M. Rossi-Wilcox and David Whitehouse, *Drawing
    Upon Nature: Studies for the Blaschkas' Glass Models*
    (Corning, NY, 2007).
10 William Firebrace, *Memo for Nemo* (London, 2016), p. 51.
11 William Beebe, *Half Mile Down* (New York, 1934).
12 Firebrace, *Memo for Nemo*, pp. 141–3.

13 Philip Pugh, 'Benthic Siphonophores: A Review of the Family *Rhodaliidae* (*Siphonophora, Physonectae*)', *Philosophical Transactions of the Royal Society of London, B: Biological Sciences*, CCCI/1105 (1983), pp. 165–300.

14 Steven H. D. Haddock and John N. Heine, *Scientific Blue-water Diving* (San Diego, CA, 2005).

15 'New Photos by Alexander Semenov Showcase the Alien Beauty of Jellyfish', www.earthporm.com, accessed January 2019.

16 See www.oceanexplorer.noaa.gov/expeditions, accessed March 2018.

5 JELLYFISH CULTURE

1 'ZooLex Exhibit Jellies', press kit details of the special exhibition *Jellies: Living Art, Monterey Bay Aquarium* (2005).

2 Satava-v-Lowry, 323 F.3d 805 (9th Circuit 2003) before: Barry S. Silverman and Ronald M. Gold (Circuit judges) and Charles R. Weinger (Senior Circuit judges).

3 Venice Biennale, Ocean City, Architect: Arup Biomimetic, www.australiandesignreview.com, accessed August 2018.

4 Woodsprite, https://aliens.fandom.com, accessed May 2018.

5 'Octonauts and the Jellyfish Bloom', www.youtube.com, accessed February 2017.

6 *Finding Nemo*, pixar.wikia.com/wiki/Jellyfish, accessed March 2017.

7 See https://en.wikipedia.org/wiki/Jellyfish_(film), accessed January 2017.

8 Arthur Conan Doyle, 'The Adventure of the Lion's Mane', from *The Case-book of Sherlock Holmes* (Ware, 1993).

9 Jules Verne, *Twenty Thousand Leagues Under the Sea* (London, 2017), p. 418.

10 Ali Benjamin, *The Thing About Jellyfish* (London, 2015).

11 Gillian Flynn, *Gone Girl* (London, 2012).

12 Margaret Atwood, *Alias Grace* (London, 2009).

13 George Crabbe, *The Poetical Works of Rev. George Crabbe*, vol. III, 'The Borough', Letter IX (London, 1834), lines 83–4.

14 Ibid., lines 87–90.

15 Guillaume Apollinaire, 'La Méduse', in *The Bestiary*, ed. Didier Alexander (Paris, 2014).

16 Mark Doty, 'Difference', in *My Alexandria* (Champaign, IL, 1995).

17 Michael Rosen, 'Jellyfish', in *Big Book of Bad Things* (London, 2010).

18 Karl Pilkington, 'Jellyfish', in *Happyslapped by a Jellyfish* (London, 2008), p. 135.

19 Natalie Harris-Spencer, 'What Jellyfish Tastes Like', https://theedibleeditor.com, 15 August 2010.

20 M. T. Pedersen et al., 'On the Gastrophysics of Jellyfish Preparation', *International Journal of Gastronomy and Food Science*, IX (2017), pp. 34–9.

21 Dany Inman, 'Invasion of the Jellyfish: Is it Time to Get Frying?' *BBC News Magazine* (3 August 2017).

6 LIGHT, DEATH AND IMMORTALITY

1 Pliny the Elder, *The Natural History of Pliny*, trans. John Bostock and H. T. Riley (London, 1855).

2 Osamu Shimomura, 'The Discovery of Aequorin and Green Fluorescent Protein', *Journal of Microscopy*, CCXVII/1 (January 2005), pp. 3–15.

3 Mats Ormö et al., 'Crystal Structure of the *Aequorea victoria* Green Fluorescent Protein', *Science*, CCLXXIII (1996), pp. 1392–5.

4 Charles Richet, 'Nobel Lecture, 1913', www.nobelprize.org, accessed September 2018.

5 Michael J. Abrams et al., 'Self-repairing Symmetry in Jellyfish through Mechanically Driven Reorganisation', *Proceedings of the National Academy of Sciences of the USA*, 112 (2015), pp. 3365–73.

6 Ferdinand Boero, 'Everlasting Life: The "Immortal" Jellyfish', *The Biologist*, LXV/3 (2016), pp. 16–19.

7 Nathanial Rich, 'Can Jellyfish Unlock the Secret of Immortality?', *New York Times Magazine* (28 November 2012).

8 A. Sánchez Alvarado and S. Yamanaka, 'Rethinking Differentiation: Stem Cells, Regeneration and Plasticity', *Cell*, CLVII/1 (2014), pp. 110–19.

9 Rich, 'Can Jellyfish Unlock the Secret of Immortality?'

10 Richard Holloway, *Waiting for the Last Bus: Reflections on Life and Death* (Edinburgh, 2018).

11 Rich, 'Can Jellyfish Unlock the Secret of Immortality?'

12 Roger Dobson, 'Jellyfish Plaster that Heals Nasty Wounds', *Daily Mail* (2 January 2018).

13 Dorothy Spangenberg, 'Development Studies of *Aurelia* (Jellyfish) Ephyrae which Developed during the SLS-1 Mission', *Advances in Space Research*, XIV/8 (1994), pp. 239–47.

7 WORLD DOMINATION

1 Jeremy B. C. Jackson, 'The Future of the Oceans Past', *Philosophical Transactions of the Royal Society of London, B: Biological Sciences*, CCCLXV/1558 (2010), pp. 3765–78.

2 Lisa-ann Gershwin, *Stung! On Jellyfish Blooms and the Future of the Ocean* (Chicago, IL, and London, 2013), p. 344.

3 The International Programme on the State of the Ocean (IPSO), http://www.stateoftheocean.org (2013).

4 'Dark Days for Estrada', www.economist.com, 18 December 1999.

5 Jacqueline Goy, 'Long-term Fluctuations of *Pelagia noctiluca* in the Western Mediterranean Sea: Prediction by Climate Variables', *Deep-sea Research*, XXXVI/2 (1989), pp. 269–79.

6 Gershwin, *Stung!*, pp. 43–57.

7 Jennifer E. Purcell, 'Jellyfish in Chesapeake Bay and Nearby Waters', NOAA, Ocean Service Education (2017).

8 Rebecca R. Helm, 'Evolution and Development of Scyphozoan Jellyfish', *Biological Review*, XCIII/2 (2018).

9 Gershwin, *Stung!*, p. 12.

10 Robert H. Condon et al., 'Questioning the Rise of Gelatinous Zooplankton in the World's Oceans', *BioScience*, LXII/2 (2012), pp. 160–69.

11 Kylie A. Pitt and Cathy H. Lucas, eds, *Jellyfish Blooms* (New York and London, 2014).

12 National Science Foundation, 'Scientists Discover Stinging Truths about Jellyfish Blooms in the Bering Sea', news release 08-088 (29 May 2008).

13 Robert H. Condon et al., 'JEDI: Jellyfish Database Initiative', www.researchgate.net, accessed September 2018.

14 Karl Mathiesen, 'Are Jellyfish Going to Take Over the Oceans?', www.theguardian.com, 21 August 2015.

15 Thomas K. Doyle, 'Ecological and Societal Benefits of Jellyfish', in *Jellyfish Blooms*, ed. Pitt and Lucas.

16 Kylie A. Pitt et al., 'The Ecology of Scyphozoan Jellyfish in Lake Illawarra', *Wetlands(Australia)*, XXI/2 (2004), pp. 116–23.

17 'North Sea Lobsters' Surprising Appetite for Jellyfish Revealed', www.scotsman.com, 28 December 2017.

18 Killian Quigley, 'Thinking Jellies', www.sydney.edu.au, 10 August 2018.

19 Jonathan Franzen, 'Why Birds Matter', *National Geographic Magazine* (January 2018).

Select Bibliography

Agassiz, Louis, *Contributions to the Natural History of the United States of America* (Boston, MA, 1862)

Ballard, Robert D., *The Eternal Darkness: A Personal History of Deep-sea Exploration* (Princeton, NJ, 2000)

Beebe, William, *Half Mile Down* (New York, 1934)

Benjamin, Ali, *The Thing About Jellyfish* (London, 2015)

Castellani, Claudia, and Martin Edwards, *Marine Plankton: A Practical Guide to Ecology, Methodology and Taxonomy* (Oxford, 2017)

Firebrace, William, *Memo for Nemo* (London, 2016)

Gershwin, Lisa-ann, *Stung! On Jellyfish Blooms and the Future of the Ocean* (Chicago, IL, and London, 2013)

—, *Jellyfish: A Natural History* (Lewes, 2016)

Gibson, Susannah, *Animal, Vegetable, Mineral? How Eighteenth-century Science Disrupted the Natural Order* (Oxford, 2015)

Goy, Jacqueline, *Les Miroirs de méduses, biological et mythologies* (Rennes, 2002)

Haeckel, Ernst, *Kunstformen der Natur* (Leipzig, 1904)

Hardy, Sir Alister C., *The Open Sea: Its Natural History Part 1: The World of Plankton* (London, 1959)

Hyman, Libbie Henrietta, *The Invertebrates*, vol. I: *Protozoa through Ctenophora* (New York, 1940)

Irmscher, Christoph, *Louis Agassiz: Creator of American Science* (Boston, MA, 2013)

Mayer, Alfred G., *Medusae of the World* (Washington, DC, 1910)

Peyssonnel, Jean-André, *Dissertation sur le corail* (Paris, 1725)

Richards, Robert, *The Tragic Sense of Life: Ernst Haeckel and the Struggle Over Evolutionary Thought* (Chicago, IL, 2008)

Russell, F. S., *The Medusae of the British Isles* (Cambridge, 1953), 2 vols

Sardet, C., *Plankton: Wonders of the Drifting World* (Chicago, IL, 2015)

Verne, Jules, *Twenty Thousand Leagues Under the Sea*, trans. Mendor T. Brunetti (London, 1994)

Wilk, Stephen R., *Medusa: Solving the Mystery of the Gorgon* (Oxford, 2000)

Williams, Peter le B., et al., *Art Forms from the Abyss: Ernst Haeckel's Images from the HMS Challenger Expedition* (London, 2015)

Winsor, Mary P., *Starfish, Jellyfish and the Order of Life* (New Haven, CT, and London, 1976)

Associations, Websites and Apps

AUSTRALIAN MARINE STINGER ADVISORY SERVICES
www.stingeradvisor.com
Information on all aspects of jellyfish with a focus on management.

BIOLUMINESCENCE
https://biolum.eemb.ucsb.edu
The website is the work of Steven Haddock and MBARI.

THE JELLYFISH APP
https://thejellyfishapp.com
Allows you to identify jellyfish worldwide. Has a facility for asking
questions of Lisa-ann Gershwin, the jellyfish expert.

MARINE BIOLOGICAL ASSOCIATION OF THE UK, PLYMOUTH
www.marlin.ac.uk
MarLin (The Marine Life Information Network) provides detailed
information on different jellyfish around the coasts of the British Isles.

MONTEREY BAY AQUARIUM RESEARCH INSTITUTE (MBARI)
www.jellywatch.org
Responsible for JellyWatch, enabling non-scientists to participate
in monitoring jellyfish populations everywhere. The website has
information on sightings and videos and facts about jellyfish.

NATIONAL OCEANIC AND ATMOSPHERIC ADMINISTRATION (NOAA)

https://oceanservice.noaa.gov

A variety of topics are covered relating to jellyfish and the oceans.

SCRIPPS INSTITUTION OF OCEANOGRAPHY

https://scripps.ucsd.edu

Information on jellyfish distribution and abundance as well as facts about jellyfish.

SIPHONOPHORES

www.siphonophores.org

A site written and maintained by Dr Casey Dunn.

SMITHSONIAN INSTITUTE

www.ocean.si.edu

Their Ocean Portal provides a good overview of jellyfish and comb jellies.

WOODS HOLE OCEANOGRAPHIC INSTITUTION

www.whoi.edu

News and updates on the ocean science, expedition blogs and the ocean's 'twilight zone'.

Acknowledgements

I owe Jonathan Burt, the series editor, an acknowledgement but also gratitude, for introducing the idea of a book on jellyfish. I am indebted to several institutions and individuals, both here and abroad.

My readers' ticket at the Bodleian, my fellowship at the Linnean Society and my visits to the Zoological Society Library in Regents Park gave me access to books, articles and images that provided me with the necessary historical perspective on the topic. Steven Haddock put me in touch with the MBARI team in America and I was also fortunate in being able to visit several authorities in Australia who are actively engaged in jellyfish research. In this connection I am much indebted to Kylie Pitt of Griffith University who generously gave up her time to show me her laboratory at Sea World, Southport. Anthony Richardson of the University of Queensland discussed with me the thorny subject of jellyfish numbers, while Bryan Fry, of the same institution, introduced me to his work on jellyfish venom. In Sydney I was lucky enough to meet Killian Quigley from the Environmental Institute, whose work on the aesthetics of the undersea proved relevant to my studies and who suggested I meet the curator of Macleay Museum, Jude Philp, on the university campus. These meetings proved very fruitful. I am also grateful to Stephen Keable, who manages the collection of invertebrates at the Australian Museum, Sydney, for showing me his stock of preserved jellyfish.

Back in the UK I was fortunate to visit one of the world's experts on siphonophores, Philip Pugh, who introduced me to lures and biolu-minescence, while I received help in understanding the role played by green fluorescent protein in brain research from Iain Robinson from the MRC National Institute for Medical Research. Two academics from

Cambridge University were helpful: Frankie Dunn, who provided information on fossil jellyfish, and Susannah Gibson, a zoophyte enthusiast. I was directed by Philip Pugh to the historian Mary P. Winsor in Canada, who kindly commented on the chapter 'A Lineage of Uncertainty' and made some useful suggestions. To my namesake in Bangor University, I owe a debt of gratitude for supplying information and images belonging to Ernst Haeckel; likewise, I am grateful to Gunnar Brehm of the Phyletische Museum in Jena for telling me more about Haeckel, the man and their collection. On an entirely different matter, Mie Pedersen provided me with information on the manufacture of jellyfish crisps which, I hope, will soon reach the supermarket shelves.

I would also like to acknowledge the help provided by two friends, both biologists, Peter Bright and Tony Gaston, who read through my script, and to Tom, my son, who helped me with the organization of the material and corrected my English. To my wife Elinor I am indebted for her support and willingness to accompany me to the other side of the world to improve my understanding of jellyfish and to swim together in the Great Barrier Reef.

I would particularly like to thank Sandra Assersohn for her assistance in seeking permissions and sourcing some of the book's images. Finally, I wish to extend my gratitude to Michael Leaman and the staff of Reaktion Books for their assistance in seeing the project through.

Photo Acknowledgements

The author and publishers wish to express their thanks to the below sources of illustrative material and/or permission to reproduce it.

Alamy: pp. 9 (Andrey Nekrasov), 104 (United Archives GmbH), 110 (Craig Lovell/Eagle Visions Photography); Alzinous: p. 59; Bigstock: p. 61 (Swims with Fish); Bodleian Library: pp. 77 left and right, 142; Bridgeman Images: p. 122 (Royal Albert Memorial Museum, Exeter, Devon, UK); Corning Museum of Glass: pp. 80, 81, 82 (Lent by Cornell University, Department of Ecology and Evolutionary Biology); Dr Shirley Cripps: p. 34; Elissaveta Dandali: p. 93; Helen Dyne: p. 98 bottom left; Friedrich Schiller University Jena: p. 96; Floodslicer: p. 102; Daniela Forti: p. 98 bottom right; Courtesy the Gesso Foundation and Sperone Westwater, New York: p. 46; Getty Images: p. 112 (DEA/ICAS94); ©David Gruber & Brennan Phillips: p. 68; Janne Hellsten (nurpax): p. 8; Tim Horn: p. 97; Howcheng: p. 111; Hübsch: p. 100; Image Quest Marine Picture Library: pp. 32, 51, 141 top and bottom (Andrey Nekrasov); Linnean Society of London: p. 22; Kgbo: p. 42; Shin Kubota: p. 127; Library of Congress, Washington, DC: pp. 18, 91, 95; Los Angeles County Museum of Art (LACMA): p. 140 (Gift of George and Lillian Kuwayama AC1999.225.1); National Oceanic and Atmospheric Administration (NOAA): p. 12 (OAR/National Undersea Research Program (NURP); 'Seas, Maps and Men'), 56, 90 (© Kevin Raskoff, California State University); Mary Evans Picture Library: pp. 35 (interfoto/ Sammlung Rauch), 84; © 2004 MBARI: p. 62 bottom left and right (Steven Haddock); Museum d'Historire Naturelle du Havre: p. 76; National Science Foundation: p. 125 (Maria Pia Miglietta); Nature Picture Library: pp. 25 (Ingo Arndt), 29

Index